106106714

Idaho

Idaho

Charles George and Linda George

Children's Press®
A Division of Grolier Publishing
New York   London   Hong Kong   Sydney
Danbury, Connecticut

Frontispiece: Sawtooth peaks

Front cover: South Fork of the Snake River

Back cover: Barns with pea fields and wheat fields near Genesee

Consultant: Judith Austin, Idaho State Historical Society

Please note: All statistics are as up-to-date as possible at the time of publication.

Visit Children's Press on the Internet at http://publishing.grolier.com

Book production by Editorial Directions, Inc.

Library of Congress Cataloging-in-Publication Data

George, Charles, 1949–
    Idaho / Charles George and Linda George.
      144 p. 24 cm. — (America the beautiful. Second series)
    Includes bibliographical references (p.) and index.
    Summary : Describes the geography, plants, animals, history, economy, religions,
culture, sports, arts, and people of Idaho.
    ISBN 0-516-21037-8
    1. Idaho—Juvenile literature. [1. Idaho.] I. George, Linda. II. Title. III. Series.
    F746.3646 2000
    979.6—dc21
                                                          99-21547
                                                          CIP

GROLIER
PUBLISHING

Acknowledgments

The authors wish to thank the former Idaho governor Philip E. Batt and his staff, Governor Dirk Kempthorne and his staff, the Idaho Travel Council, and the Idaho State Historical Society for their help in securing research materials for this book. Special thanks go to Beverly Cownover and the staff of the interlibrary loan office at Baylor University Library in Waco, Texas, and to Brenda Perkins and the staff at the Brownwood Public Library.

Sun Valley

Idaho Falls

Beaver Pond

Mountain bluebird

Contents

Farming

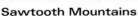

Sawtooth Mountains

A farmer's market

Bighorn sheep

CHAPTER ONE

A Gem of a State

Idaho is known for its breathtaking scenery.

A rubber raft, guided by adventurers eager to test their skills against the rapids, slices between boulders on the majestic Snake River. Shouts of triumph echo through the canyon as the raft advances to the next rapids. The landscape surrounding the river is breathtaking. This is Idaho.

The northwestern part of the United States is known for spectacular scenery that includes white-water rapids, snow-capped peaks, steep canyons, and some of the most beautiful lakes on Earth. Nowhere is this more true than in Idaho—the Gem State.

The shape of Idaho, which resembles a frying pan, represents decades of history and political maneuvering. With its diverse geography, personality, and economy, Idaho can be viewed as several states in one. Idaho's fierce regionalism has caused difficulties, but it has also been important to the state's prosperity.

Opposite: Autumn in the Grand Targhee National Forest

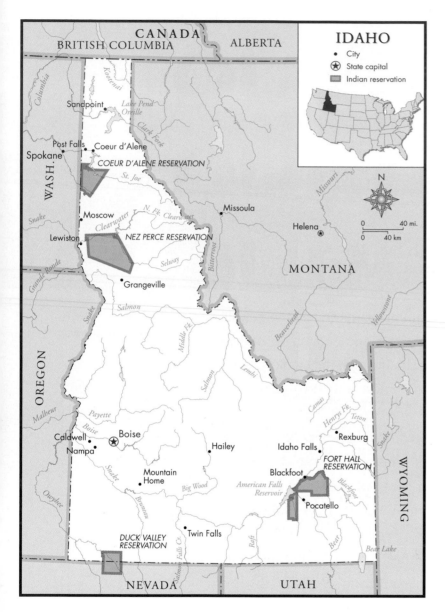

Geopolitical map
of Idaho

The Name *Idaho*

The name *Idaho* was originally suggested for the Colorado Territory in 1860, but the U.S. Congress rejected it a year later. *Idaho* is not an Indian word, but Western poet and journalist Joaquin Miller (1837–1913) may have written about a Shoshone Indian exclamation, *E-dah-how*, in newspaper articles from the 1860s. The word is believed to mean "it is sunup!" or "gem of the mountains." Some historians think a member of the U.S. Congress made up an Indian-sounding word for the territory. Others credit a steamboat operator with inventing the name. In any case, the territory was named Idaho officially in 1863.

Idaho's landscape is as varied as any state, with 3 million acres (1,215,000 hectares) of wilderness area. Packhorses are required to reach some parts of the state. Craters of the Moon National Monument looks like a moonscape, with extinct volcanoes and lava flows dating to ancient

times. The southern part of the state, once arid desert, is now fertile, productive farmland, thanks to the introduction of irrigation.

One of Idaho's most impressive attractions is the mighty Snake River, winding through Hells Canyon along the Idaho-Oregon border. Hells Canyon is the deepest canyon in North America. To the north lies Lake Coeur d'Alene, one of the world's most beautiful lakes. No matter where you venture in the state, you'll find people who love where they live and appreciate the natural beauty of their home—"the gem of the mountains"—Idaho.

Tennessee walker horses at home in Swan Valley

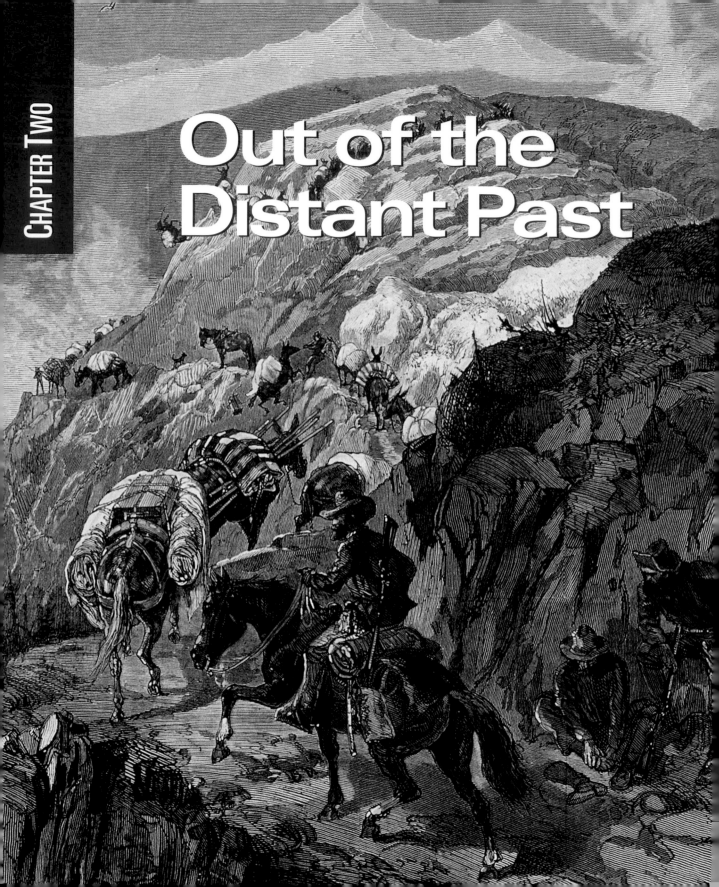

CHAPTER TWO

Out of the Distant Past

Idaho's forests provided food and shelter for Native Americans.

Native Americans arrived in the land now known as Idaho about 13,000 years ago. The Kutenai, the Pend d'Oreille, the Coeur d'Alene, the Nez Perce, the Paiute, the Shoshone, and the Bannock lived in the region.

Earliest Inhabitants

Historians believe the first people in Idaho had ancestors from Asia. It is thought that these ancestors walked across the Bering land bridge from Asia to North America. They followed large game animals and killed them with primitive weapons. The artifacts of these early inhabitants include hunting tools and pottery fragments. Eventually, these early Idahoans took up residence in caves and rock shelters.

Forests and lakes formed by glacier melt led Pacific Coast tribes to relocate to the northern part of today's Idaho. There they found plenty of game and starchy bulbs to eat.

Opposite: The Nez Perce being pursued on Dead Mule Trail, 1877

To the south, in the Snake River area, the Shoshone also migrated to find food throughout the year. In late autumn, using traps and weirs, Shoshone fishers caught salmon by the thousands. Weirs are enclosures set in a river to trap fish. The Indians dried and smoked the fish on wooden racks to use as nourishment when food was sparse. During the winter months, dried meats and leeks ground into flour were stored in pits lined with grass and leaves.

Native Americans created petroglyphs as messages and records of their events.

Early Art

Prehistoric rock art has been found all over Idaho. Petroglyphs—symbols carved into rock walls and boulders—and pictographs—designs painted on rock—have been discovered on the western Snake River plain and in the Owyhee uplands in southwestern Idaho. These carvings or paintings were used to mark trails, record important events, or communicate with the spirits.

Horses

Exploring the Southwest in the 1500s and 1600s, Spanish explorers brought the horse to North America. This amazing animal changed the way of life of Idaho's Native Americans and paved the way for enormous advancements in hunting and mobility.

The use of horses for transportation and hunting spread northward from the Southwest. Trade increased among both local and distant tribes. Unfortunately, new diseases that were carried, such as smallpox, by the Europeans, were also passed along. Many thousands of American Indians who had no immunity to the European diseases died as a result.

Some Indian groups in the state did not fully accept the use of the horse, however. The Nez Perce and Lemhi Shoshone bred horses on a limited basis. The Boise and Bruneau Shoshone, who lived in the mountains, preferred traveling on foot. They felt horses would compete with the game animals for available food.

Horses changed the lives of Native Americans in many ways.

Indian Tribes of Idaho

The Shoshone lived in the southern part of the state, along the Snake River plain and in nearby river valleys and highlands. Today, many Shoshone live near Pocatello, on the Fort Hall Indian Reservation, which they share with the Bannock people.

The Bannock, a group of northern Paiute, moved into eastern Idaho from southeastern Oregon after they learned to ride horses. The Bannock and the Shoshone living together are called Sho-Bans. Many Shoshone and Paiute now live in the Duck Valley Indian Reservation on the Idaho-Nevada border south of Boise.

The Nez Perce occupied the area from the Clearwater River into northeastern Oregon and southeastern Washington. They have a reservation located east of Lewiston. The name *Nez Perce*, which means "pierced nose" in French, was given to the tribe because some of them wore nose pendants. They called themselves *Ne-Mee-Poo*, or "the people."

Northern Idaho provided a home for other Native American groups, including the Coeur d'Alene, the Pend d'Oreille, and the Kutenai. Their reservations are in the states of Montana and Washington. ■

Appaloosa horses were bred by the Nez Perce and are still a part of Idaho.

An Annual Rendezvous

An enormous benefit of having horses was being able to get together once a year with other tribes. This intertribal meeting, or rendezvous, was held near what is now Weiser in Treasure Valley. The highlight of the monthlong event was a great salmon run. And while storerooms were filled with salmon for the coming winter, participants performed ceremonial dances, gambled, and traded.

The Nez Perce bred and traded the distinctive Appaloosa ponies. The Shoshone traded buffalo hides and dried meat, while the Umatilla, from the Pacific Coast, brought shells from the ocean. Arrowheads were traded by the Paiute of Oregon. During the rendezvous, all territorial disputes were forgotten so that everyone could trade.

Eventually, white traders and mountain men, or trappers, learned of the rendezvous and came to trade too. Permanent trading posts were eventually established.

Exploring the West

Meriwether Lewis and William Clark left St. Louis, Missouri, on May 14, 1804, to explore the vast area that the United States had bought from France in the Louisiana Purchase of 1803. The first white men ever to explore this new territory entered Idaho through Lemhi Pass in August 1805.

Unable to go any farther, Lewis and Clark backtracked, went farther north, then reentered through Lolo Pass. With the help of the Shoshone and the Nez Perce, they traveled down

Exploration of Idaho

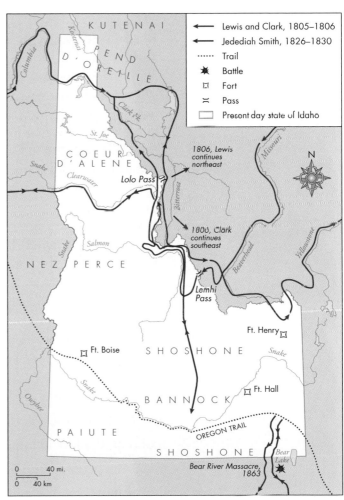

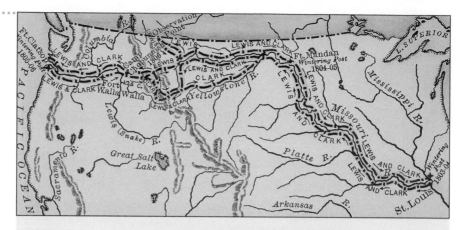

The Lewis and Clark Expedition

After the Louisiana Purchase in 1803, President Thomas Jefferson gave Meriwether Lewis and William Clark the task of exploring the new land—from St. Louis, Missouri, all the way to the Pacific Ocean. They set off in May 1804, with a team of about three dozen men skilled in practical trades or the sciences.

After following the Missouri River, they wintered with the Mandan Sioux in present-day North Dakota. They continued their journey in the spring of 1805.

An interpreter and his wife, a young Shoshone named Saca-jawea, accompanied them. With their help, Lewis and Clark identified landmarks and passed peacefully through Indian lands.

They crossed the Continental Divide into Idaho through Lemhi Pass in the Bitterroot Range. Following the Lemhi River north to the upper Salmon River, they crossed back into Montana near modern-day Missoula, then into Idaho again through Lolo Pass. From Lolo Pass, they moved steadily westward, reaching the Pacific Ocean by the second week of November. They returned to St. Louis on September 23, 1806. ■

the Clearwater and Snake Rivers in dugout canoes to the Columbia River and the Pacific coast. They didn't come back through Idaho until 1806. On their trip, they recorded valuable information about the people, animals, and plants. They also sketched maps of their route.

Sacajawea (1786?–1812)

A Shoshone, Sacajawea was born in the Bitterroot Mountains near present-day Salmon, Idaho. A party of Minnetaree Indians captured the young Sacajawea and traded her to the Hidatsa tribe. From there, she was either purchased or won in a wager by Toussaint Charbonneau, a French-Canadian fur trader living with the Hidatsa. Sacajawea became one of his wives.

Charbonneau met Lewis and Clark when they visited Idaho in 1805 and was hired as an interpreter. Clark wrote in his journal, "The wife of Shabono [Charbonneau] our interpreter we find reconciles all the Indians as to our friendly intentions—a woman with a party of men is a token of peace."

With Sacajawea's help, amiable relations were established with the Shoshone. The tribe provided Lewis and Clark with horses and guides before their exploration of the Columbia River. While negotiating for supplies and safe passage, Sacajawea recognized the Shoshone chief. He was Cameahwait, her brother! Considered a valued member of the Lewis and Clark expedition, Sacajawea is believed to have died in 1812. ■

News of the area's wildlife—beaver, otter, and other fur-bearing animals—traveled quickly. Fur trappers rushed into the Northwest and set up forts to ease travel and exploration. Other people also moved into the once sparsely populated region.

Trappers and Trading Posts

John Colter (1775?–1813), an explorer who traveled with Lewis and Clark, left the party on the return trip to travel on his own. He crossed the headwaters of the Missouri and Yellowstone Rivers three times between 1806 and 1810. From Idaho's Teton Valley region and the area that later became Yellowstone National Park, he relayed reports of geysers and hot springs. His stories led people to call the area Colter's Hell.

The lower falls of the Yellowstone River, which John Colter crossed in his travels

John Jacob Astor did much to promote the fur industry in the West.

In 1809, British-Canadian trapper and surveyor David Thompson established Kullyspell House, the first trading post in Idaho, at Lake Pend Oreille. Thompson explored extensively along the United States–Canada border, in upper parts of the Columbia River system, during the few years Kullyspell House was in business.

Fort Henry, near what is now St. Anthony, was another settlement. In 1810, Blackfoot Indians fought Andrew Henry and a group of trappers, driving them across the Continental Divide. They established a winter headquarters at Henry's Fork.

In Wyoming the following spring, a group of westbound traders sponsored by wealthy New York fur tycoon John Jacob Astor encountered Henry's settlement. The Astor group eventually reached the Pacific coast and established Astoria, a post at the mouth of the Columbia River. They

Jedediah Smith (1799–1831)

Born in what is now Bainbridge, New York, Jedediah Smith moved to St. Louis, Missouri, as a teenager. He became a hunter, explorer, and mountain man. A Christian, Smith never used tobacco, alcohol, or profane language. One of his first expeditions involved tracing the Columbia River from its source to its mouth. He explored the Lemhi, Teton, and Cache Valleys, as well as the Boise, Payette, and Weiser regions.

At first, Smith wanted to make a profit and a name for himself. Later on, his goals changed, and he encouraged mining, lumbering, and agriculture. Smith was killed by Comanche on the Santa Fe Trail in 1831. He is considered one of Idaho's great explorers. ■

bought furs and shipped them across the Pacific to China. Unprepared for the wilderness, these men endured attacks from Indian tribes, disease, and hunger. The British took over Astoria in 1813.

The Hudson's Bay Company of Great Britain established Fort Nez Perces at the junction of the Columbia and Snake Rivers. It flourished from 1820 until 1832. Trappers from the Henry's Fork area, including Donald Mackenzie, Jim Bridger, and Jedediah Smith, competed for beaver pelts.

Horses carrying fur-trade supplies

In 1822, the American-owned Rocky Mountain Fur Company was established. Between 1825 and 1840, an annual summer rendezvous was held. It was an opportunity for traders and trappers to meet and exchange goods.

Because of the success of the rendezvous, Nathaniel Wyeth, an American merchant, established Fort Hall on the Snake River in 1834, and travelers and traders met there for the next twenty years. Another fort that flourished was Fort Boise, constructed by the Hudson's Bay Company at the junction of the Boise and Snake Rivers. When fashionable Europeans began wearing silk instead of fur, the fur trade eventually declined.

Spreading the Gospel

In 1831, the Nez Perce contacted William Clark in St. Louis. They requested he send teachers and textbooks, so that their people could be educated. Clark misinterpreted this as a request for missionaries to spread the gospel among the Native Americans. Within three years, Methodist missionaries had relocated to Fort Hall.

In 1836, Presbyterian missionaries Henry and Eliza Spalding joined the Methodists and established a mission at Lapwai, Idaho. Marcus and Narcissa Whitman and Sarah and Asa Bowen Smith, who taught the Nez Perce near Kamiah, on the Clearwater River, soon followed.

Missionary Henry Spalding influenced the Nez Perce.

Spalding also taught the Nez Perce to farm. A church, school, water-powered sawmill, flour mill, and blacksmith shop were erected. Spalding also acquired a printing press for printing the Gospel of John in the Nez Perce language, so that the Native Americans could read it for themselves. Asa Smith compiled a Nez Perce dictionary. The Spaldings abandoned Lapwai after the Whitmans were killed by Cayuse Indians in Washington in 1847.

Another settlement, the Mission of the Sacred Heart in the Coeur d'Alene area, was established in 1842 by Father Pierre Jean De Smet, a Jesuit missionary, on the St. Joe River. The mission was subject to flooding and was moved to higher ground in 1850. Constructed in Greek Revival style, the mission still stands near Cataldo, east of Coeur d'Alene. It is the oldest building in Idaho.

A new religious group entered the West in 1848 when Brigham Young led the Mormons to what is now Salt Lake City, Utah. In the 1850s, Mormons moved into southeastern Idaho. Missionaries who came to Idaho succeeded in spreading the Christian faith through this new territory, paving the way for more pioneers.

The lure of gold brought many people west.

The Discovery of Gold

When Elias Pierce discovered gold on Orofino Creek in 1860, settlers quickly moved into the region. In less than a year, tent and log-cabin cities sprang up all along the Clearwater River. Lewiston became a major transportation port on the river and provided a service center for mining camps.

A larger gold strike occurred in August 1862 on Grimes Creek, about 200 miles (322 kilometers) south of the Clearwater strike. As a result, Idaho City soon became the largest city in the Pacific Northwest, with a population of more than 6,000 by 1863.

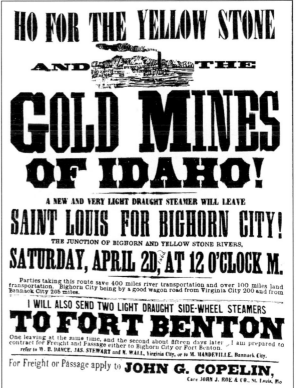

HO FOR THE YELLOW STONE

AND THE

GOLD MINES OF IDAHO!

A NEW AND VERY LIGHT DRAUGHT STEAMER WILL LEAVE

SAINT LOUIS FOR BIGHORN CITY!

THE JUNCTION OF BIGHORN AND YELLOW STONE RIVERS,

SATURDAY, APRIL 2D, AT 12 O'CLOCK M.

Parties taking this route save 400 miles river transportation and over 100 miles land transportation. Bighorn City being by a good wagon road from Virginia City 200 and from Bannack City 205 miles.

I WILL ALSO SEND TWO LIGHT DRAUGHT SIDE-WHEEL STEAMERS

TO FORT BENTON

One leaving at the same time, and the second about fifteen days later. I am prepared to contract for Freight and Passage either to Bighorn City or Fort Benton.

refer to W. B. DANCE, JAS. STEWART and N. WALL, Virginia City, or to M. MANDEVILLE, Bannack City.

For Freight or Passage apply to JOHN G. COPELIN,

Care JOHN J. ROE & CO., St. Louis, Mo

Historical map of Idaho

Territorial Status

In 1863, the U.S. Congress granted Idaho territorial status. Idaho Territory included a large portion of modern Montana and Wyoming, with Lewiston as the first territorial capital.

By 1864, when the boundaries of the state were redrawn to their present locations, the capital had been moved to Boise. A part of western Wyoming remained in Idaho Territory until 1868. Boise got its name early in the century from French-Canadian trappers, who had just crossed the desertlike area to the southeast and saw the woods—*bois*—along

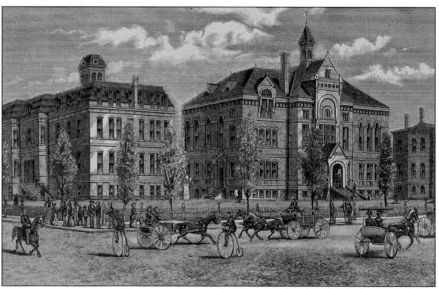

By the late 1800s, Boise was becoming a bustling city.

the river. Boise, a service center for mining camps, was established after the Grimes Creek gold strike in 1862.

Conflict with the Indians

Angry over losing their lands to white settlers, the Coeur d'Alene joined other tribes in 1858 and resisted attempts to confine them on reservations. The U.S. Army fought back without mercy. Horses and food supplies were taken or destroyed. As many as 400 Shoshone were killed in 1863 at the Bear River Massacre. It was the worst violence between the army and Idaho's Native Americans. In 1878, Chief Buffalo Horn led the Bannock into war against settlers in the Snake River valley. They, too, failed to drive away the whites.

The most famous confrontation between the U.S. Army and local tribes was the Nez Perce War of 1877. An 1863 treaty between the Nez Perce and the military said that the tribe must live on a reservation only one-tenth the size of their previous lands. A group of Nez Perce, led by Chief White Bird of the lower Salmon River, south of Grangeville, and Chief Joseph of the Oregon Wallowa Valley, west of Hells Canyon, refused to accept the treaty.

More than a dozen years later, in 1877, the U.S. Army gave Chief White Bird and Chief Joseph a final order—they had one month to comply with the treaty. As their answer to the order, a few warriors from White Bird's group murdered four white settlers. Consequently, the Battle of White Bird Canyon took place on June 17, 1877. Thirty-four soldiers died in the fighting. No Nez Perce were killed.

Chief Joseph (1840?–1904)

In-mut-too-yah-lat-lat or "Thunder Rolling Down the Mountain" was known to whites as Chief Joseph. He was born in the Wallowa Valley in what is now Oregon. A peace-loving man, he led 750 of his people 1,500 miles (2,414 km) toward Canada, fleeing U.S. Army troops in 1877. The Nez Perce were forced to surrender in October 1877. The heartrending speech Chief Joseph gave has often been quoted:

I am tired of fighting. Our chiefs are killed. . . . The old men are all dead. . . . It is cold, and we have no blankets. The little chil-dren are freezing to death. My people, some of them, have run away to the hills. . . . I want to have time to look for my children, and to see how many of them I can find; maybe I shall find them among the dead. Hear me, my chiefs: My heart is sick and sad. From where the sun now stands, I will fight no more forever.

Chief Joseph was held prisoner until 1885, when he was allowed to return to the Northwest. Chief Joseph urged his people to avoid drinking and gambling and to educate themselves. He died in 1904. ■

Fearing retaliation from the U.S. Army, the Nez Perce requested sanctuary from the Crow in northern Montana and ran for their lives—and for freedom. The cavalry caught up with them on July 11 near Kamiah, Idaho, forcing the tribe down the Lolo Trail to the Bitterroot Mountains. Eventually, they reached Big Hole Valley in Montana, but a militia was waiting in ambush. They killed eighty-three Nez Perce, including fifty-three women and children.

The tribe then moved to the southeast, through the Lemhi Valley and Island Park areas and across Targhee Pass, until they reached the newly founded Yellowstone National Park. Tourists ran from the approaching Indians, fearing for their lives. Joseph tricked army troops into believing he had headed south, toward Wyoming. Instead, he led his people across Montana, hoping to find sanctuary in Canada. The cavalry overtook them at Bear's Paw, only 42 miles (68 km) from the Canadian border.

White Bird and 100 members of his tribe continued into Canada and settled there, but Chief Joseph surrendered to U.S. Army troops, unwilling to force additional hardship on his people. They were taken to Indian Territory (now Oklahoma), where they remained until 1885. Eventually, 150 of the Nez Perce were allowed to return to a reservation in the state of Washington. Joseph went with them. He died in 1904, having kept his vow to "fight no more forever."

The surrender of Chief Joseph in 1877

Silver Mining

Gold wasn't the only thing drawing people to Idaho. Silver was discovered in Hailey in the Wood River valley in 1880, bringing new settlers into the territory. Hailey soon became the richest town in Idaho. A major silver strike in 1885 further boosted Idaho's economy.

The mining of silver required railway lines and smelters, unnecessary for gold mining. Investors were not hesitant, though, to pay for these improvements, as they recovered their investments in record time. Kellogg, Osburn, and Wallace flourished as industrial mining communities. Spokane, Washington, served as a major shipping center for the area.

Statehood!

The economic boost from silver helped push Idaho to statehood. A constitution, adopted in 1889, preceded statehood. On July 3, 1890, Idaho became the forty-third state. The state's first governor was George L. Shoup. President Benjamin Harrison was to have signed the bill into law on July 4, but Idaho representatives opted to have the bill signed a day earlier. They had learned that a new state's star was added to the U.S. flag on the first Independence Day after the territory became a state.

George L. Shoup

By 1890, political parties had been established in the state, and the first legislative and state elections were held. The new state's population in 1890 was 88,548. The Great Northern Railroad Reserve Act, which passed that year, provided for railroad construction connecting St. Paul, Minnesota, and Seattle, Washington, through northern Idaho. Eventually, a network of roads and railroads crisscrossed the state, hauling freight and gold and silver from the mountains.

Problems encountered during Idaho's twenty-seven years as a territory would continue into the next century. These problems included political disputes that arose when lawmakers in Washington, D.C., tried to impose their will on the independent Idahoans. Growing opposition to the Mormon presence in the state, increasing development in communication and transportation, and fierce competition over Idaho's rich mineral deposits plagued the newly formed state as the twentieth century dawned.

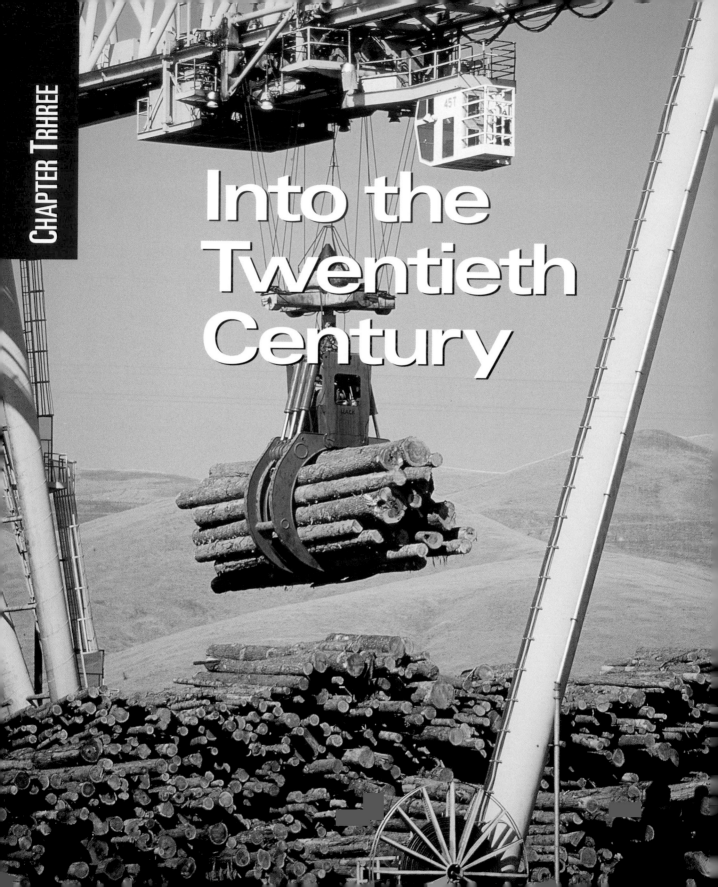

CHAPTER THREE

Into the Twentieth Century

n its early years as a state, five key events affected Idaho. First was the founding of the University of Idaho at Moscow, on October 3, 1899. Selecting this site for the university represented the state legislature's desire to link northern and southern Idahoans through the pursuit of higher education. Northern Idahoans had expressed their desire to become part of the state of Washington or to form a new state. The legislature hoped to placate the separatists with the new university.

Idaho's participation in the Columbian Exposition in Chicago in 1893 was the second event to affect Idaho greatly. The exposition commemorated the 400th anniversary of the arrival of Christopher Columbus in the Americas. The Idaho Building's frontier

The Idaho State Building at the 1893 Columbian Exposition

Opposite: Logs at a Lewiston paper mill

design and materials distinguished it at the exposition. Gold, silver, zinc, lead, and other metals mined in Idaho were displayed, along with equipment used to extract these resources from the land. The effort required to plan and construct the exhibit unified Idahoans.

The third important event was the elimination of the anti-Mormon Test Oath required to vote or to hold public office. Mormons were not allowed to vote prior to 1895 because their religion permitted the practice of polygamy—being married to more than one spouse at one time.

Giving women the right to vote in 1896 was the fourth key event. Women were subsequently elected to public office, and their impact on state government increased.

The fifth important event was the organization of the first Idaho Regiment of Infantry Volunteers. After the United States declared war on Spain on April 25, 1898, President William McKinley issued a call for volunteers. Idaho's response marked its first participation in national governmental affairs.

Governor Frank Steunenberg of Idaho passed along the call and 672 volunteers reported to Camp Stevenson in Boise for training. Colonel John W. Jones, publisher of the *Idaho News* in Blackfoot, led the troops. The war lasted only 113 days, but thirty-four Idahoans were killed in military service during the Spanish-American War.

Conservationism

Idahoans have always disagreed about the proper use and handling of natural resources. Native Americans had used nature's bounty to survive and live in harmony with the land, not to increase personal

The lumber industry took a toll on Idaho's tree supply.

wealth or political power. But an entirely new philosophy arrived with the white settlers.

Most Americans at that time considered the country's natural resources to be almost limitless. Fur trappers killed beavers to excess and lumbermen felled trees by the thousands. Water drawn from rivers for irrigation turned deserts into farmland, but the riverbeds eventually dried up. After a while, farmers realized they had to cooperate and share water for mutual benefit.

The discovery of gold, silver, lead, and other minerals in the

The Industrial Workers of the World

The Industrial Workers of the World, founded in Chicago in 1905, was a labor union established to work for higher pay and better working conditions for its members. William D. "Big Bill" Haywood (left), one of the founders, wanted one big union of members from many industries. Union tactics included strikes (workers refusing to work), slowdowns (workers refusing to work at peak efficiency), sabotage (workers creating problems for their employers through destruction), and collective bargaining (workers talking directly with their bosses about wages and working conditions).

Haywood wanted to bring socialism—governmental control of private enterprise—to the United States. The Industrial Workers of the World lost power in the 1920s, but workers in lumber camps benefited from the improvements the union made in working conditions. ■

Rocky Mountains led to greed and violence among settlers of the American West. Miners disregarded farmers and ranchers and destroyed the land—and one another—in their search for riches.

Clashes in the Mines

Disagreements between mine workers and mine owners led to many violent encounters. As the cost of shipping ore by rail increased, prices for silver and other ores dropped. When miners demanded higher wages, mine owners cut wages even further. Owners then fired union miners and hired nonunion laborers called "scabs" to work in the mines. Armed guards protected the scabs from out-of-work union miners, but there were several incidents of bloodshed.

On July 11, 1892, a gunfight and a dynamite explosion occurred at the Frisco Mine in Gem, near Wallace, killing six miners and injuring twenty-five. Under martial law, state and federal troops restored order. Approximately 300 miners and union sympathizers were held in prison camps called bullpens for two months. Trials resulted in two dozen union leaders being held accountable for the violence.

While in prison, the union leaders created the Western Federation of Miners. Upon their release, they spread the word among Coeur d'Alene mine owners, encouraging them to increase wages to union scale—$3.50 for a ten-hour day.

The 1892 explosion at the Frisco Mine

The Bunker Hill and Sullivan Company refused. The result was an attack on the Bunker Hill complex at Wardner on April 29, 1899. The Dynamite Express—train cars filled with 3,000 pounds (1,362 kilograms) of dynamite—rammed into the complex. Much of the mine's heavy equipment and many buildings were destroyed. The event was dubbed the Second Battle of Bunker Hill—a reference to the Revolutionary War battle.

Governor Frank Steunenberg summoned federal troops. All over the Coeur d'Alene area, men were arrested and placed in bullpens. Charged with murder, conspiracy, and arson, some of the prisoners were held without trial for almost two years. Eventually, thirteen men were tried, and ten were convicted, fined, and imprisoned.

Martial law continued until 1901. Scabs or immigrant workers from other states replaced union miners, stripping the union of power. But the miners were far from defeated.

On December 30, 1905, the former governor Frank Steunenberg left his home. As he opened the gate in his front yard, a bomb exploded and killed him. In 1906, union member Harry Orchard confessed to the murder.

Orchard also implicated three other union leaders—William D. "Big Bill" Haywood, George Pettibone, and Charles Moyer. The group of three immediately fled to Colorado. Detectives followed them to Denver and brought them back to Boise for trial. The murder trials attracted national attention. Orchard was tried in 1907, found guilty, and sentenced to die. Because he testified against the other men, however, Orchard's sentence was reduced to life in prison.

Senator William E. Borah of Idaho prosecuted Haywood, Pettibone, and Moyer in separate trials. Clarence Darrow represented the defendants. Tall, with broad shoulders, Darrow specialized in dramatic oratory. The jury acquitted Haywood due to lack of evidence. Pettibone was later acquitted, and the charges against Moyer were dropped.

Three men accused of murdering Governor Steunenberg are shown here: Mr. and Mrs. George Pettibone (left), William Haywood (center), and Mr. and Mrs. Charles Moyer (right)

Irrigating the Idaho Desert

In 1895, a law providing for the use of public water for irrigation was passed. Arid areas in southern Idaho could now be farmed by using water from the Snake River. Crops replaced sagebrush. Idaho Falls, Blackfoot, Pocatello, American Falls, and other river towns prospered.

Three agricultural events influenced Idaho's history in the first decades of the twentieth century. First, the National Reclamation Act, supplying federal aid for irrigation, passed in 1902. Second, water rights were granted to farmers along the Boise River in 1906. And third, by 1920, prices for crops fell. The decline caused economic hardship.

Sheep and Cattle

Cattle ranchers and sheep ranchers waged constant battles over open-range grazing rights. In February 1896, two sheep ranchers who ventured into cattle country in Cassia County were killed for trespassing. The main suspect in the murders was Jack "Diamondfield" Davis, known as a swaggering storyteller and braggart.

Davis was tried for murder. The jury of mostly sheep ranchers and farmers found him guilty and the judge sentenced him to death by hanging. Davis's lawyer, James H. Hawley, won him a reprieve. Reviewed by the U.S. Circuit Court of Appeals, Davis was again found guilty and condemned to die. In the summer of 1901, Hawley managed to get a second reprieve for his client.

William E. Borah (1865–1940)

Born in Illinois in 1865, William E. Borah arrived in Idaho in 1890 and lived there for fifty years. As Idaho's senator for more than thirty years, Borah was known as a fair, honest, and intelligent politician. He attracted national attention when he prosecuted "Diamondfield" Davis and "Big Bill" Haywood.

Borah felt concern for Idaho's major natural resources, including water, soil, and forests. He steadfastly pursued land reclamation and conservation, supported by federally funded projects. Borah also wanted a graduated income tax, national prohibition (making it illegal to sell or consume alcoholic bever-ages), and direct election of senators.

After World War I (1914–1918), Borah opposed President Woodrow Wilson's proposal of an international forum—the League of Nations—to work out problems between nations and draw the countries of the world into a mutually beneficial coalition. Borah felt that U.S. membership in the League of Nations would dilute U.S. power in world politics and economics. Borah also opposed a federal law allowing women to vote, feeling that each state should make that decision for itself. Borah's oratory attracted positive attention to Idaho and its citizens. He died in 1940. ■

Eventually, Davis was granted a pardon. He left for Nevada and became a rich, respectable miner. Jack Davis was killed by a taxi in Las Vegas in 1949.

Economics and Politics

Idaho became politically progressive during the first decade of the twentieth century. Citizens decided it was time to save what was left of the state's natural resources. In 1906, William E. Borah was elected to the first of six terms in the U.S. Senate. Borah worked to establish national forests, irrigation projects, regulation of hunting and fishing, and the creation of fire patrols in Idaho forests.

Dams

One controversial irrigation project involved construction of the American Falls Dam on the Snake River. When the dam was completed, the town of American Falls had to be moved. After the reservoir filled, the only visible structure was "the lonely grain elevator sticking up like a tombstone for the town."

The demand for irrigation grew. The Twin Falls Land and Water Company, created in 1905 by Ira B. Perrine, used water from the Snake River to irrigate tens of thousands of acres. In 1906, the U.S. Bureau of Reclamation built the Minidoka Dam, adding 100,000 acres (40,500 ha) of available farmland.

The Minidoka project also increased production and use of electric power. By 1920, the Minidoka Dam helped generate electricity for more than 1,000 farm families.

The Great Depression

Farmers prospered during the first two decades of the twentieth century, since food demands during World War I meant higher prices for crops and land. Farmers borrowed money for operating expenses during the war, upgrading from horses and horse-powered tools to mechanical farming methods.

At the war's end, however, they couldn't repay their loans. The 1920s were hard on Idaho's farmers. Agriculture fell into a slump that lasted through the Great Depression of the 1930s, and Idaho's economy collapsed.

During the 1930s, the federal government established agencies to provide jobs for millions of unemployed workers. The Civilian Conservation Corps provided work in Idaho's forests, conserving and maintaining resources. The 1930s also saw progress in construction of state highways—another source of jobs for Idahoans.

World War II

Japan's surprise attack on Pearl Harbor in Hawaii, on December 7, 1941, led many white Americans to view Japanese Americans and Japanese immigrants as potential enemies. Japanese Americans were sent to relocation camps to separate them from the rest of the population. Those from Idaho, Oregon, and Washington were interred at Camp Minidoka, near Twin Falls, and offered the opportunity to work on farms, filling in for farmworkers in the armed forces.

When the United States entered World War II (1939–1945), Idaho's economy began to recover from the depression. Miners, farmers, and factory workers produced metals needed to make weapons, food, and parts for airplanes, guns, and ammunition. Air bases in Boise, Pocatello, and Mountain Home trained men and women for the war effort.

Before the war, Idaho's economy had been largely agricultural, with the majority of its population in rural areas. Gradually, the economy moved to manufacturing and food processing, and

many Idahoans moved to urban areas. By 1960, one-half of Idaho's citizens resided in cities.

New highways and other roads were constructed in the 1930s and 1940s.

Nuclear Energy

The federal government contributed to Idaho's postwar economic boom. Pend Oreille Lake was selected for training submarine crews and testing nuclear submarines. In 1949, the Atomic Energy Commission initiated the National Reactor Testing Station, where

Idaho National Engineering and Environmental Laboratory

West of Idaho Falls is the Idaho National Engineering and Environmental Laboratory (above), once called the National Reactor Testing Station. Created on March 20, 1949, by the Atomic Energy Commission, fifty-two reactors were built and tested on the 870-square-mile (2,253-sq-km) site.

The laboratory's projects include electric vehicles, biotechnology, and lasers. Public support for the installation and its projects is mixed. Some Idahoans worry about radioactive waste contaminating the Snake River aquifer. An aquifer is a band of rock, sand, or gravel deep in the earth containing water that can be pumped to the surface. Critics' fears were confirmed in 1988 when the U.S. Department of Energy declared the laboratory one of the most contaminated nuclear-weapons sites in the nation. Since then, Idaho has tried to get permission from the federal government to transport nuclear and other hazardous waste to disposal sites in other states. ■

nuclear reactors were built. A model reactor was built at this station for the USS *Nautilus*, the world's first nuclear-powered submarine. On December 20, 1951, nuclear energy generated electricity at the station for the first time, and on July 17, 1955, Arco, Idaho, became the first town in the world to be powered completely by nuclear energy—for one hour.

CHAPTER FOUR

Toward the New Millennium

Since World War II, Idahoans have concentrated on conserving natural resources and resolving disputes between conservationists and advocates of industrial growth. Land preservation conflicts with development of mineral deposits, harvesting lumber from forestland, maintaining ranches and farms, and producing electricity with hydroelectric power. The challenge is to find ways to do both.

Idaho has worked hard to maintain its beauty and natural resources.

Wilderness Preservation

A central figure in Idaho's efforts to deal with natural resources was Senator Frank Church, who promoted passage of the National Recreation Area Act in 1962. The law was designed to preserve and expand recreation opportunities in America. In Idaho, two national recreation areas were created—the Sawtooth area in 1972 and Hells Canyon in 1976.

Opposite: The Sawtooth National Recreation Area

Church supported conservation of natural resources, but he also felt those resources should benefit Idahoans. Many times, Church ended up dueling with both preservationists—advocates for Idaho's wilderness areas—and those who wanted to make full use of natural resources.

Senator Church lost support in the state's mining, timber, and grazing regions because of his work on the 1964 Wilderness Act. This law protects wilderness areas on federal land. No roads or buildings may be built in these areas and timber harvesting is forbidden. In Idaho and Montana, more than 1.3 million acres (526,500 ha) became the Selway-Bitterroot Wilderness Area. The territory explored by Lewis and Clark was included.

One of the biggest controversies between conservationists and industrialists concerned building dams for hydroelectric power. Church was instrumental in the construction of three dams in Hells Canyon on the Snake River. Later, he supported a ban on building in that area to preserve wild areas near the river.

Protecting Birds

Nearly 500,000 acres (202,500 ha) surrounding the Snake River was designated the Snake River Birds of Prey National Conservation Area in 1980. This preserve provides a home for more raptors—birds of prey—than any other preserve in the world. More than 800 pairs of migrating peregrine falcons and ospreys, owls, northern harriers, prairie falcons, turkey vultures, kestrels, hawks, and golden eagles (left) live in the area.

Also there is the World Center for Birds of Prey, founded in Kuna in 1984 for breeding endangered hawks, falcons, owls, and eagles. Twenty-two species of more than 4,000 birds have been successfully raised and released into places as far away as the Philippines and Madagascar. ■

Environmentalists versus Industrialists

Hells Canyon National Recreation Area and Wilderness

All through Idaho's history, groups determined to use natural resources to the fullest extent have argued with environmentalists equally determined to save resources for future generations. Each group had valid reasons for its beliefs.

Hundreds of jobs are provided for Idahoans by the lumber industry, yet harvesting trees deprives wildlife of their habitat. Some species are endangered and could become extinct if their homes are destroyed.

Mining companies employ thousands of workers, but they also inflict major environmental damage. Idaho has experienced some

Frank Church (1924–1984)

Born in Boise in 1924, Frank Church served Idaho as a U.S. senator for three terms. His main contribution was in foreign policy. Appointed to the Foreign Relations Committee, Church also served on the U.S. delegation to the United Nations. Church chaired the Committee on Aging and promoted civil rights legislation in the 1960s. He also favored federal aid for education and a balance between conservation and use of natural resources. Before Frank Church died of cancer in 1984, the River of No Return Wilderness Area was renamed the Frank Church/River of No Return Wilderness Area to honor the senator's work for Idaho's wilderness areas. ■

of the worst pollution in the United States because of waste products from mining operations.

An intense debate occurred when the American Smelting and Refining Company announced its intentions to mine for molybdenum on 740 acres (300 ha) in the White Cloud Mountains using open-pit mining techniques. Open-pit mining destroys the landscape by removing whole mountains or digging huge pits to extract valuable minerals from hard rock. After heated debate and controversy, the conservationists triumphed, thanks to Governor Cecil D. Andrus and U.S. Senator Frank Church.

The Cost of Progress

Dams constructed in Idaho were not always beneficial. Catastrophe struck on June 5, 1976, when an earthen dam on the Teton River collapsed, spilling 80 billion gallons (303 billion liters) of water southward across the land. Sugar City, Rexburg, Idaho Falls, and other communities suffered enormous damage and destruction of property. About 300,000 people fled their homes. Eleven people were killed, and thousands were left homeless. Damages totaled more than $500 million.

The 305-foot (93-meter) dam collapsed because of basic design flaws and faulty construction. To prevent another such tragedy, construction techniques were scrutinized intensely and building standards were raised.

Other Disasters

On October 28, 1983, an earthquake measuring 7.3 on the Richter scale shook Idaho, killing two children and causing $4 million in damages. With its epicenter in the Lost River valley, the earthquake was the strongest in the continental United States in twenty-four years.

Investigating the damage after the 1983 earthquake

Drought came to Idaho in 1987 after an unusually arid winter. As a result, the worst forest fires since 1910 raged in 1989, burning thousands of acres in the south-central part of the state. The town of Lowman was partially destroyed. The worst forest-fire seasons in the state's recorded history occurred in 1992, after five years of drought, and again in the summer of 1994, when wildfires consumed another estimated 750,000 acres (303,750 ha) of Idaho's forests.

One of the state's worst tragedies occurred on May 2, 1972, at the Sunshine Mine in Kellogg. Fire broke out in the mine below the 3,100-foot (946-m) level and acrid smoke filled the tunnels. Many miners survived, but ninety-one were killed.

Economics and Government

In the 1950s, major industries in Idaho grew dramatically, in spite of disputes among the citizens of Idaho and between Idaho and the federal government. Citizens wanted federal funds for projects such as the National Reactor Testing Station in Arco, the Bureau of Reclamation's Palisades and Anderson Ranch Dams, and the U.S. Army Corps of Engineers' Lucky Peak and Dworshak Dams, as well as for reclamation and power projects and the improvement of highways in Idaho.

Idahoans were adamant, though, about maintaining the freedom of private enterprises to manage conservation of natural resources. They refused to relinquish local control of farming, food processing, transportation, tourism, hydroelectricity, mining, and lumber to federal authorities.

Regionalism

Regionalism—the different opinions and interests of citizens in various parts of the state—affects cultural development, community life, business, and industry. Mining and lumbering are closely linked to those areas of Idaho closest to the states of Washington and Montana. Northern Idaho is part of the so-called Inland Empire, between the Cascades and the Rocky Mountains, while the southeastern part of the state, with substantial Mormon settlement, leans toward Salt Lake City, Utah.

Radical Groups in Idaho

Over time, Idaho has become a gathering place for radical conservative groups known as survivalists. These groups oppose governmental aid or protection, which they consider a burden rather than a benefit. Survivalists believe in being completely self-sufficient—from raising or growing their own food to home-schooling their children. Some believe so strongly in their right to live independently that they are willing to defend that right with deadly weapons. A few militant white supremacist groups, who feel white people are superior to other races, have also settled in Idaho.

The founder of Aryan Nations—Richard Butler—chose the Idaho Panhandle when he came from California in the 1970s. He wanted a place where his group could establish a fortified compound for what he felt were troubled times ahead. He selected a site near Hayden Lake, 10 miles (16 km) from Coeur d'Alene, for his 20-acre (8-ha) compound. His people learned guerrilla war tactics and urban terrorism. Butler has been called "the elder statesman of American hate." ■

The Siege of Ruby Ridge

Randy Weaver (above) belonged to an anti-government, white-supremacist religious group called Christian Identity. In 1992, the federal government charged Weaver with weapons violations. Weaver refused to appear in court and took refuge in far northern Idaho. In a remote mountain cabin on Ruby Ridge, Weaver, his wife, their children, and a friend of the family made a stand.

In 1992, agents from the Federal Bureau of Investigation and the Bureau of Alcohol, Tobacco, and Firearms surrounded the cabin. During several gun battles, three people were killed — one federal agent and Weaver's wife and son. The standoff continued for another ten days, until Weaver surrendered and was charged with numerous crimes. The Ruby Ridge siege has become one of the rallying points for similar extremists. ■

Looking to the Future

With enormous pride, Idaho celebrated 100 years of statehood in 1990. The Gem State looks forward to the future, hoping to exceed its goals. Leonard J. Arrington, the author of a history of Idaho, put it eloquently: "Idaho will remain a state where young people can still dream dreams, reach out to nature and each other, and see visions of a more perfect society. . . . Idaho offers opportunity to use and not abuse, to reclaim and restore the great gifts that nature bestows upon all its creatures."

**Idaho's centennial
celebration in 1990**

CHAPTER FIVE

Diverse Landscapes

daho is located in the northwestern United States. Washington and Oregon border it to the west, Montana and Wyoming to the east, the Canadian province of British Columbia to the north, and Nevada and Utah to the south.

Rivers, lakes, and streams make up almost 1 percent, 823 square miles (2,132 sq km), of the state's total surface area. Idaho's greatest length, north to south, is 486 miles (782 km). Due to its unusual shape, which some have compared to a capital letter *L*, the state's width east to west varies from 285 miles (459 km) in the south to only 45 miles (72 km) in the north. This narrow northern area is called the Panhandle.

Idaho offers dramatic cliffs and deep canyons.

Opposite: Fly-fishing at Beaver Pond

Geologic History

Idaho's unusual boundaries provide a variety of dramatic land formations: mountain peaks above 12,000 feet (3,660 m) high, canyons as deep as 8,032 feet (2,450 m), rugged lava flows, and vast deserts. The region has a unique geologic history. Millions of years of continuous upheaval caused by earthquakes, volcanic eruptions, and glacial ice packs formed this diverse landscape. Hundreds of millions of years ago, Idaho was part of the shoreline of a vast continent, as evidenced by a layer of ocean sediment found beneath parts of the Panhandle.

During the Mesozoic era, 250 million years ago, mountain ranges were pushed up from the earth by molten granite rising from below. The rock cooled to form strips of silica containing gold, silver, and other precious metals that later drew people to the state and gave it the nickname the Gem State.

Over the millennia, Idaho's landscape has been altered drastically. Vast glacial lakes formed, remained for centuries, and then were destroyed by geologic forces. During the last 7 million years of the Miocene epoch, in the Cenozoic era, a huge body of water now called Lake Idaho covered the southwestern part of the state. Seismic changes caused this lake to be drained.

Topographical map of Idaho

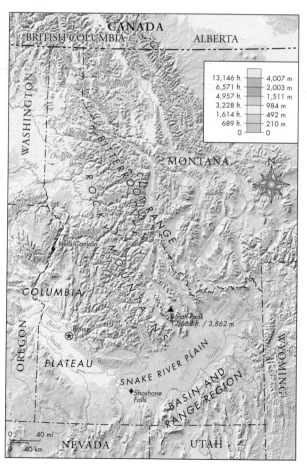

Most fossils found in Idaho are 225-million-year-old Paleozoic sea creatures and 5-million-year-old Pliocene mammals. Woolly mammoths lived along the shores of Lake Idaho along with saber-toothed tigers and other mammals, including a zebralike animal known as the Hagerman horse.

About 30,000 years ago, melting ice from glaciers formed the vast Bonneville Lake, which covered parts of Idaho, Wyoming, and Utah. Its demise caused tremendous flooding in southern Idaho. Still another flood, the Spokane flood, helped carve out areas of northern Idaho about 20,000 years ago.

Geographic Regions

Because of its size and location, Idaho contains parts of four major geographic regions of the western United States. The northern Rockies cover most of the Panhandle and central Idaho. The Columbia Plateau extends along the Snake River plain in the south and southwest and along the western border almost to Coeur d'Alene Lake in the north. A small, triangular section of southeastern Idaho is located in the Great Basin region, and just to the east, along the Wyoming border, there is a narrow section of the middle Rockies.

The Northern Rockies

Most of northern Idaho—almost half the state's area—is part of the northern Rockies region, including most of Idaho's mountain ranges. Idaho has more than 200 mountain peaks that rise 8,000 feet (2,400 m) or higher. The Bitterroot and the Beaverhead Mountains form much of the state's border with Montana. Other mountain

Sunrise over the
Sawtooth Mountains

Mount Borah

ranges divide the state, forming what locals call the central wilderness. They are the Lemhi Range, the Lost River Range, and the Sawtooth Mountains.

Borah Peak, or Mount Borah, the state's highest point at 12,662 feet (3,862 m), is just north of Mackay. It was named for William E. Borah, Idaho's U.S. senator for many years. To the west lie the Salmon River Mountains and the Seven Devils.

This region also boasts the deepest canyon in North America—Hells Canyon on the Snake River. Hells Canyon National Recreation Area and Wilderness surrounds the nearly 70-mile (113-km)-long gorge through which the Snake River passes.

The Columbia Plateau

Most of southern Idaho, along with the area around Lewiston and Moscow in the west, is part of the Columbia Plateau. Much of this geographic region follows the Snake River plain across the state.

The Snake River plain begins northeast of Idaho Falls, where the Snake descends from the Caribou Range. From there it follows a crescent-shaped path across southern Idaho. Volcanic flow and the erosive power of the Snake River created the plain. The underlying layers of basaltic lava are particularly visible at Craters of the Moon National Monument. Volcanic eruptions covered this 83-square-mile (215-square-kilometer) area about 15,000 years ago. National Aeronautics and Space Administration (NASA) once used the area for astronaut training, believing it to be similar to the moon's surface.

A lava rock at Craters of the Moon National Monument

Ice Caves

Idaho has several ice caves. Two of the most spectacular are Shoshone Ice Caves, north of Twin Falls in south-central Idaho, and Crystal Ice Cave, north of American Falls.

The Shoshone Ice Caves (left), Idaho's most famous underground caverns, contain a glacier that measures 1,000 feet (305 m) long and 40 feet (12 m) high. The caves provided a cool respite from desert heat for Shoshone travelers before the arrival of Europeans in Idaho. Pioneers, who quarried ice to preserve food, discovered these caves in 1880.

In Crystal Ice Cave, stalagmites as tall as 16 feet (5 m) rise from a lake of pure ice. Water trickles into the cave, 155 feet (47 m) beneath the earth's surface, then freezes into these unusual ice formations. ■

In southwestern Idaho, the Snake River turns northward, extending along the Columbia Plateau to north of Weiser. The area southwest of a line from Boise to Twin Falls is called the Payette section. It contains a maze of canyons, mesas, buttes, and terraces, and includes the Owyhee Mountains.

North of the Salmon River Mountains, along Idaho's border with northeastern Oregon and southeastern Washington, is another part of the Columbia Plateau. This section, called the Walla Walla Plateau, surrounds Lewiston and Moscow. Characterized by a thick, fertile layer of fine silt called loess, this region of rolling hills and relatively low elevations—710 feet (217 m) to 3,000 feet (915 m)—is also referred to as Palouse Country. Idaho's lowest point is in this region.

The Great Basin

The triangle-shaped area of southeastern Idaho called the Great Basin is actually part of the Basin and Range Province that covers much of Utah and Nevada. This desertlike area south of Pocatello contains basins of sand and gravel separated by six mountain ranges, the largest of which is the Pocatello-Bannock.

The Middle Rockies

The middle Rockies portion of Idaho forms the state's border with Wyoming. These mountains, including the outlying ranges of the Tetons and the Wasatch, form a belt extending north and south along the border. The largest ranges in the area are the Caribou and Bear River Ranges. Mountains in these ranges rise to between 7,000 feet (2,135 m) and 10,000 feet (3,050 m).

Rivers and Lakes

Idaho has more than 16,000 miles (25,744 km) of rivers and streams, thousands of natural lakes, and numerous large, man-

Idaho's Geographical Features

Total area; rank	83,574 sq. mi. (216,457 sq km); 14th
Land area; rank	82,751 sq. mi. (214,325 sq km); 11th
Water area; rank	823 sq. mi. (2,132 sq km); 31st
Inland water; rank	823 sq. mi. (2,132 sq km); 25th
Geographic center	Custer, southwest of Challis
Highest point	Borah Peak, 12,662 feet (3,862 m)
Lowest point	Snake River at Lewiston, 710 feet (217 m)
Largest city	Boise
Population; rank	1,011,986 (1990 census); 42nd
Record high temperature	118°F (48°C) at Orofino on July 28, 1934
Record low temperature	−60°F (−51°C) at Island Park Dam on January 18, 1943
Average July temperature	67°F (19°C)
Average January temperature	23°F (−5°C)
Average annual precipitation	19 inches (48 cm)

The Snake River is the longest in Idaho.

made reservoirs. With the exception of Bear River, which drains southeastward into Utah's Great Salt Lake, all of Idaho's rivers flow into the Columbia River and on to the Pacific Ocean.

The longest and most economically important river in the state is the Snake. Beginning near the Continental Divide in Wyoming's Yellowstone National Park, it flows across Idaho and turns north, eventually leaving the state at Lewiston. Before joining the Columbia River near Pasco, Washington, the Snake travels 1,038 miles (1,670 km) from its source.

Fishers and white-water rafters love the Snake for its abundant game fish as well as its thrilling rapids. The river also brings life to the arid regions in the center of the state, where farmers depend on it for irrigation and ranchers to water their livestock. The Shoshone referred to it as the River of the Sagebrush Plain. Idaho's cities also depend on the Snake for

Shoshone Falls

About 5 miles (8 km) from the city of Twin Falls is one of the most stunning sites in Idaho. Shoshone Falls (left), cascading 212 feet (65 m), is higher than Niagara Falls by 45 feet (14 m), and known nationwide as the Niagara of the West. These thundering, horseshoe-shaped falls, 1,000 feet (305 m) wide, are the biggest tourist attraction of the Snake River canyon. ■

water. Fourteen dams along the river provide hydroelectric power for homes and industries.

As it crosses the state, the Snake is interrupted numerous times by dams and the reservoirs they create. Downstream from Palisades Dam in far-eastern Idaho is the American Falls Dam, near Pocatello. The American Falls Reservoir is the state's largest man-made lake.

Two of the state's major rivers—the Salmon and the Clearwater—flow only in Idaho. The Salmon is often called the River of No Return because travelers could not navigate upstream against its currents. It begins in the Sawtooth Mountains and flows so swiftly that only expert white-water rafters will brave its rapids. Today, only jet-powered boats are able to make the return trip upriver. Much calmer than the Salmon is the Clearwater, a favorite for trout fishing. The Middle Fork of the Salmon and the Middle Fork of the Clearwater were included in the original group designated wild and scenic rivers under 1968's Wild and Scenic River Act.

Winter on the Salmon River

Along the Clearwater River

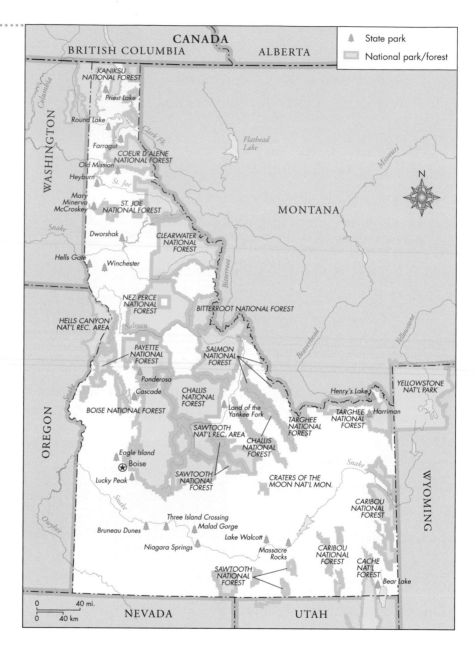

Idaho's parks and forests

Many other rivers are important to Idaho. In the north are the Kootenai, Pend Oreille, and Spokane. Farther south, the St. Joe and Coeur d'Alene provided an important route for early settlers and loggers. Two unusual rivers in central Idaho flow out of the

Henry Dworshak (1894–1962) and Dworshak Dam

Henry Dworshak of Burley moved to Idaho from Minnesota when he was thirty years old. He published the *Burley Bulletin* and was elected U.S. representative in 1938. He won a special election to fill the seat of Senator John Thomas. Dworshak lost his reelection bid in 1948 but later returned to office when his opponent, Bert H. Miller, died a year after being elected. Appointed to finish Miller's term, Dworshak was reelected in 1954 and 1960 and served until his death in 1962.

Beginning in 1959, the Dworshak Dam (above) was constructed across the North Fork of the Clearwater River. The dam, named for Senator Dworshak, is the tallest and largest straight axis dam in North America. A straight axis dam is neither concave (curved inward) nor convex (curved outward). The dam was completed in 1973. ■

Lost River Range. The Big Lost River and the Little Lost River disappear into a lava formation and do not reemerge for 120 miles (193 km).

Many of Idaho's rivers flow into the state's natural lakes, which number more than 2,000. Most of these are small, isolated mountain lakes, but several are large.

A marina on Lake Pend Oreille

The largest, Lake Pend Oreille, covers 148 square miles (383 sq km) in the Panhandle. Other major natural lakes include Priest, Hayden, and Coeur d'Alene. Coeur d'Alene is said to be one of the most beautiful lakes in the world. Lovely Payette Lake lies in the central part of the state near McCall. To the east and southeast lie Henry's Lake and Bear Lake.

Trees and Plants

Some 40 percent of Idaho's land is forested, including one of the nation's largest and finest western white pine forests. An astonishing variety of trees cover the state's mountains and valleys. Evergreens include Douglas fir, Engelmann spruce, lodgepole pine, white fir, and hemlock. A forest of red cedars on the west side of Priest Lake contains trees thought to be 2,000 years old. Hardwood trees such as birch, maple, aspen, and willow line the valley streams.

A huge variety of shrubs, grasses, and wildflowers also thrive in the state. Some of the most common include the syringa, dogwood, chokecherry, huckleberry, mountain heath, and ocean spray. Rabbitbrush and sagebrush grow in the desert areas of southern Idaho.

Hundreds of kinds of wildflowers bloom in Idaho. Some of the most common are columbine, larkspur, violet, buttercup, and lily. The bloom of the syringa, or mock orange, is the state flower.

A forest of snow-covered Douglas fir trees

Wildlife

Idaho's forests and plains are teeming with wildlife. The mountains boast several varieties of big game, including deer, elk, bighorn sheep, moose, and mountain goats. The dense forests are also home to predators such as cougars, bobcats, black and grizzly bears, and timber wolves.

Smaller animals also find shelter in the state's forests. Fur-bearing animals such as beaver, muskrat, mink, and otter share the

Many bighorn sheep make their home in Idaho.

habitat with weasels, marmots, and squirrels. Rockier, drier regions are home to coyotes, badgers, gophers, jackrabbits, and antelopes.

Bird species abound in Idaho. Ducks, geese, herons, egrets, and whistling swans populate mountain lakes. Ring-necked pheasants, quail, chukar partridges, and mourning doves are popular with sportsmen. Hundreds of species of songbirds nest throughout the state, and bald eagles, golden eagles, and various other birds of prey find sanctuary in the canyons.

Game fish thrive in Idaho's rivers, lakes, and streams. Rainbow trout are the most common, but cutthroat, speckled, brown, golden, and Dolly Varden trout also swim in the state's waterways. In addition, perch, bass, bluegill, crappie, salmon, and catfish tempt local anglers.

Weather

Idaho's climate is as varied as its geography. The mountain ranges surrounding the state determine much of its weather conditions. Moist Pacific air comes across Washington and Oregon, but much of the rain falls before reaching Idaho. The mountains along the eastern border with Montana and Wyoming protect much of the state from the Arctic cold those states usually experience in winter.

Precipitation varies from area to area. Some parts of the state, including much of the Snake River plain, receive less than 10 inches (25 centimeters) of rainfall per year. Other areas, particularly in the mountains of central and northern Idaho, receive more than 50 inches (127 cm). Average annual precipitation is 19 inches (48 cm).

A warm, sunny day in an Idaho meadow

Annual average temperatures also vary across the state. The average temperature in July is 67° Fahrenheit (19° Celsius). The average temperature in January is 23°F (–5°C). However, the area around Lewiston, in northwest Idaho, is warmer and has a much longer growing season (the period of frost-free days) than locations at higher elevations hundreds of miles to the south and east.

Parts of the most isolated central region, at extremely high elevations, have a growing season of less than two months. The Lewiston area, much of the Snake River plain, and even as far north as the city of Coeur d'Alene, enjoy growing seasons of 120 to 200 days each year.

Record highs and lows reflect the role elevation plays in Idaho's climate. The state's hottest temperature on record, 118°F (48°C), was measured on July 28, 1934, at Orofino, east of Lewiston. The coldest day ever recorded in the state was –60°F (–51°C), at Island Park Dam on January 18, 1943. Island Park is just south of Reynolds and Targhee Passes, which cross the Continental Divide into Montana just west of Yellowstone National Park.

CHAPTER SIX

Four States in One

The plains of south-west Idaho

daho is said to be like four states within a single border. North-ern Idaho is part of an Inland Empire with Spokane, Washington, 16 miles (26 km) west of Idaho, as the center. Idahoans in this section identify more closely with the state of Washington than with Idaho.

Boise, the capital, serves as the center for the southwestern section of the state. Included in this section are industrial and agricultural areas extending into eastern Oregon.

Mormon culture, centered in Salt Lake City, Utah, about 100 miles (161 km) south of the Idaho-Utah border, extends into southeastern Idaho. The only section without ties to surrounding states is south-central Idaho, which is populated by business people and farmers who try to promote unity among the other three sections of the state.

Opposite: Autumn near Boise

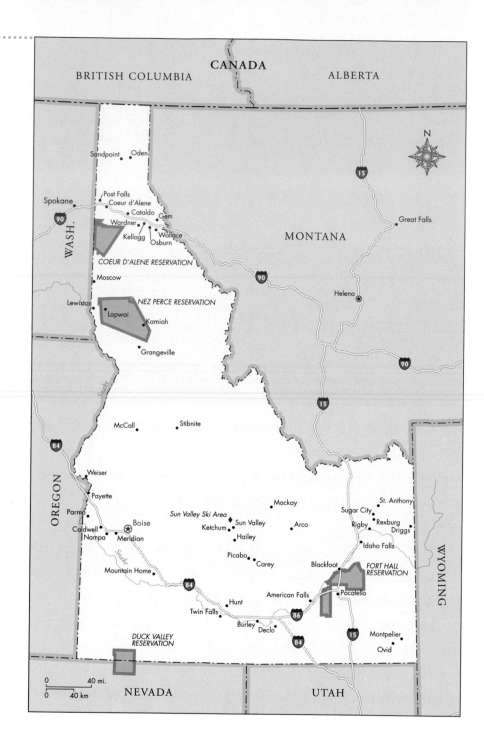

CANADA

BRITISH COLUMBIA   ALBERTA

N

Sandpoint   Oden

15

Post Falls
Coeur d'Alene
Spokane
Cataldo   Gem
90
Wardner   Wallace
WASH.
Kellogg   Osburn
Great Falls
COEUR D'ALENE RESERVATION
MONTANA

Moscow
90

Lewiston   NEZ PERCE RESERVATION
Lapwai   Kamiah
Helena
Grangeville
15

McCall   Stibnite

84
Weiser
OREGON
Payette
Mackay   St. Anthony
Parma   Sun Valley Ski Area   Sugar City   Rexburg
Boise   Ketchum   Sun Valley   Arco   Rigby   Driggs
Caldwell   Hailey
Nampa   Meridian   Idaho Falls
Picabo   Carey   WYOMING
Mountain Home   Blackfoot   FORT HALL
RESERVATION
84   American Falls   Pocatello
Hunt
Twin Falls   86
Burley   Declo   15   Montpelier
DUCK VALLEY   84   Ovid
RESERVATION

0   40 mi.
0   40 km
NEVADA   UTAH

Idaho's cities and interstates

74 IDAHO

Northern Idaho

Between the Salmon River and Canada, northern Idaho enjoys a mild Pacific climate. The region includes dense forests, swift rivers, and glacial lakes. Ancient cedars and hemlocks, ferns, and white pines beautify the landscape. The area's history includes miners, farmers, and loggers who grew rich on seemingly endless natural resources.

Southwestern Idaho

As the Snake River meanders across southwestern Idaho for 500 miles (805 km), the vast plain tilts westward before narrowing near Weiser. The Snake heads north into Hells Canyon, marking the state's border for more than 100 miles (161 km).

Valleys in the southwest enjoy a mild climate, thanks to lower elevation. Most of the state's people live in this region, where fur traders and prospectors once camped and established towns. Afterward, as the twentieth century dawned, farmers, ranchers, and lumbermen settled in the area. Eventually, high-tech industries established facilities there, boosting the economy.

Central Idaho

From Idaho's southern border with Utah and Nevada, all the way to the Salmon River in the north, lies central Idaho. The Frank Church/River of No Return Wilderness Area, one of the largest in the United States, and several national forests are located in this section, along with the Sawtooth Mountains, the Boulder Mountains, the Smoky Mountains, the Pioneer Mountains, and the Lost

Hells Canyon and the Seven Devils

The deepest gorge in North America, averaging 1 mile (1.6 km) deep, is Hells Canyon on the Idaho-Oregon border. Carved over thousands of years by the Snake River, the canyon plunges 8,032 feet (2,450 m) at its deepest point—1/3 mile (0.5 km) deeper than the Grand Canyon. Hells Canyon is also one of the narrowest canyons in North America.

Hells Canyon is home to a variety of large birds, as well as bighorn sheep, deer, elk, mountain goats, cougars, coyotes, and black bears. Before Lewis and Clark explored the area at the beginning of the nineteenth century, the canyon was a hunter's paradise for Native Americans. Native Americans lived in the canyon as early as 8,000 years ago—as evidenced by rock carvings and inscriptions found in the area.

Seven Devils Mountain, in the center of the Hells Canyon Wilderness, provides the best observation point for Hells Canyon. Nez Perce legends claim the father of their race—Coyote—dug Hells Canyon in a single day to protect his people from the evil Seven Devils. ■

River Range. Ghost towns, such as Custer, Sawtooth City, Vienna, Leesburg, and Bonanza, represent the mass departures that occurred when the gold and silver ran out.

A house in one of the ghost towns near the Sawtooth Mountains

Magic Valley, another name for the Snake River valley, enjoys agricultural prosperity as its 2.5 million acres (1 million ha) of farmland contribute beans, grain, hay, potatoes, and sugar beets to Idaho's economy. Enough commercial trout are also raised there to make Idaho the top producer in the United States.

A potato field near Bruneau

Sagebrush in Camas County

Southeastern Idaho

Explorers, fur traders, and travelers on the Oregon Trail crossed through southeastern Idaho as pioneers moved steadily west. These pioneers were the first Europeans to see the Snake River plain, the Teton Valley, and the Bear Lake country. This area includes all the geographic features of the state, making it a microcosm of the land, features, and people of Idaho. Mountains, forests, waterfalls, farmland, desert, sand dunes, and scattered communities are all found in southeastern Idaho.

A State Full of Surprises

Idaho offers an amazing variety of landscapes. Farmland, streams, lakes, rivers, sagebrush desert, and mountains—some

Idaho's Hot Springs

The first summer resorts in the state were established in the late nineteenth century at Hailey and Guyer Hot Springs. The Oregon Short Line Railroad extended into the Wood River valley in the 1880s, and Hailey Hot Springs became Idaho's first real summer resort. Not long after, the waters of Guyer Hot Springs were declared "good for all nervous complaints, rheumatism, skin and blood affectations." Some people said the healing properties of the spring came from the beauty of the mountain retreat. The serenity of the mountains helped citizens cope with the stress of establishing the new state. ■

of them covered in forests—are all only an hour or so away from anywhere in the state. With highlands and lowlands, metropolitan areas and ghost towns, and people who value their independence above all else, Idaho is a great place to visit—or to live.

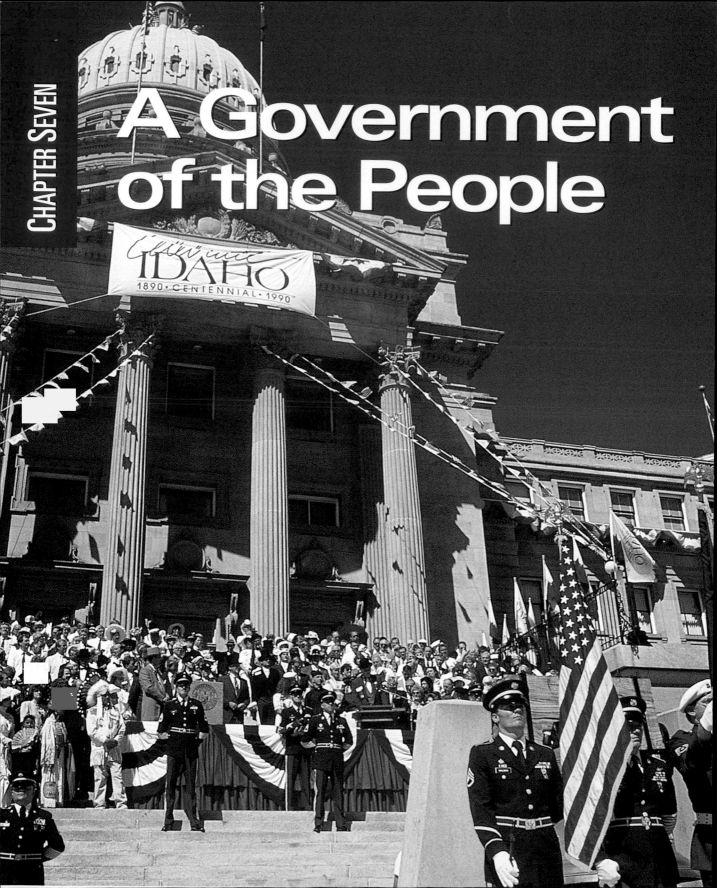

CHAPTER SEVEN

A Government of the People

Inside the house of representatives

daho adopted a constitution in 1889, almost a year before joining the Union. The state still uses that document today, though
more than 100 amendments have been added. A vote of two-thirds
of the state legislature is required to amend the constitution. It can
also be amended through a convention called by the legislature. A
state election must be held and a two-thirds majority of the state's
voters must approve the amendment for it to be incorporated into
the state constitution.

Like most other U.S. states, Idaho has three branches of government: the executive, the legislative, and the judicial. The executive branch takes care of day-to-day operations of the state's
business, proposes legislation, and enacts laws passed by the legislative branch. Courts make up the judicial branch, which inter-
prets and reviews laws and tries civil and criminal cases.

Opposite: Celebrating
the centennial at
Idaho's capitol

Idaho's State Capitol

Idaho's statehouse in Boise was built between 1905 and 1920 at a cost of $2.3 million. Constructing the same building would cost more than $100 million today. And some materials used in its construction could not be found now. One of these is the scagliola—an imitation ornamental marble made from finely ground gypsum mixed with glue.

J. E. Tourtelloutte served as architect for the project. Although Idaho's capitol is modeled after the U.S. Capitol in Washington, D.C., it has a unique feature—a geothermal well. Geothermal heat comes from the earth. Five blocks from the capitol is a well from which hot water is pumped to heat the building and the capitol mall area.

The capitol dome is topped by a solid-copper, bronze-plated eagle standing 5 feet 7 inches (1.7 m) tall, and weighing 250 pounds (114 kg). The top of the eagle is 208 feet (63 m) above the ground floor.

A 15-foot (5-m) bed of river gravel forms the base for the building's foundation, which was constructed with huge blocks of sandstone. These blocks weigh as much as 10 tons each and were moved to the site from a quarry at Table Rock by Idaho Penitentiary convicts. The interior of the building was made of four types of marble: red marble from Georgia, black marble from Italy, green marble from Vermont, and gray marble from Alaska. ∎

Idaho's State Government

Executive Branch

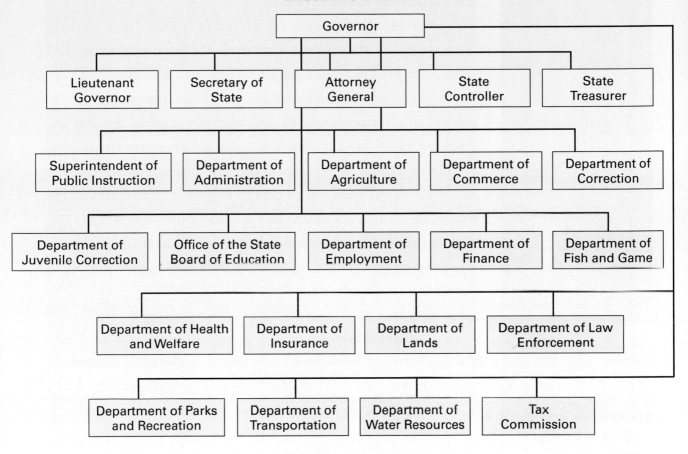

Governor

Lieutenant Governor | Secretary of State | Attorney General | State Controller | State Treasurer

Superintendent of Public Instruction | Department of Administration | Department of Agriculture | Department of Commerce | Department of Correction

Department of Juvenile Correction | Office of the State Board of Education | Department of Employment | Department of Finance | Department of Fish and Game

Department of Health and Welfare | Department of Insurance | Department of Lands | Department of Law Enforcement

Department of Parks and Recreation | Department of Transportation | Department of Water Resources | Tax Commission

Legislative Branch

Senate | House of Representatives

Judicial Branch

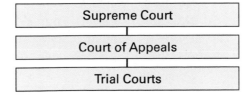

Supreme Court

Court of Appeals

Trial Courts

Executive Branch

The governor of Idaho heads the executive branch. He or she may not serve more than two four-year terms. In Idaho, as in some other states, the governor cannot appoint top state officials. The lieutenant governor, secretary of state, controllor, treasurer, superintendent of public instruction, and attorney general are elected. Each serves a four-year term with a maximum of two terms.

The lieutenant governor takes over for the governor when he or she is out of the state, ill, or unable to perform the duties of the office. The lieutenant governor also chairs the state senate. The attorney general represents the state in legal matters and in court. The attorney general is the highest legal officer in the state.

Idaho's Governors

Name	Party	Term	Name	Party	Term
George L. Shoup	Rep.	1890	Barzilla W. Clark	Dem.	1937–1939
N. B. Willey	Rep.	1891–1893	C. A. Bottolfsen	Rep.	1939–1941
William J. McConnell	Rep.	1893–1897	Chase A. Clark	Dem.	1941–1943
Frank Steunenberg	Dem.	1897–1901	C. A. Bottolfsen	Rep.	1943–1945
Frank W. Hunt	Dem.	1901–1903	Charles C. Gossett	Dem.	1945
John T. Morrison	Rep.	1903–1905	Arnold Williams	Dem.	1945–1947
Frank R. Gooding	Rep.	1905–1909	C. A. Robins	Rep.	1947–1951
James H. Brady	Rep.	1909–1911	Len B. Jordan	Rep.	1951–1955
James H. Hawley	Dem.	1911–1913	Robert E. Smylie	Rep.	1955–1967
John M. Haines	Rep.	1913–1915	Don Samuelson	Rep.	1967–1971
Moses Alexander	Dem.	1915–1919	Cecil D. Andrus	Dem.	1971–1977
D. W. Davis	Rep.	1919–1923	John V. Evans	Dem.	1977–1987
Charles C. Moore	Rep.	1923–1927	Cecil D. Andrus	Dem.	1987–1995
H. C. Baldridge	Rep.	1927–1931	Philip E. Batt	Rep.	1995–1999
C. Ben Ross	Dem.	1931–1937	Dirk Kempthorne	Rep.	1999–

Governor Dirk Kempthorne (1951–)

Dirk Kempthorne, Idaho's thirtieth governor, was born in 1951. He graduated with a degree in political science from the University of Idaho in 1975. Ten years later, in 1985, Kempthorne was elected mayor of Boise, Idaho's largest city and the state's capital. He served two terms, during which time he was chosen Citizen of the Year by the *Idaho Statesman*, the state's largest daily newspaper. In 1992, he was elected to represent Idaho in the U.S. Senate, serving on several committees including the Armed Services Committee. In 1998, he was elected governor of Idaho and left the Senate. ■

Official records of the state are kept by the secretary of state. The controllor and treasurer maintain the state financial records. The superintendent of public instruction is in charge of the Idaho school system.

Legislative Branch

In Idaho, thirty-five senators and seventy representatives in the state legislature represent thirty-five legislative districts. Each district's voters elect one senator and two representatives for each two-year term, with a four-term maximum.

The legislature meets annually, beginning on the Monday that falls on or nearest January 9. Each regular session lasts about ninety days, with no set number of days designated by law. Special sessions, limited to twenty days each, may be called by the governor.

Judicial Branch

Idaho's courts make up the judicial branch of the state government. The state supreme court, Idaho's highest court, consists of a chief

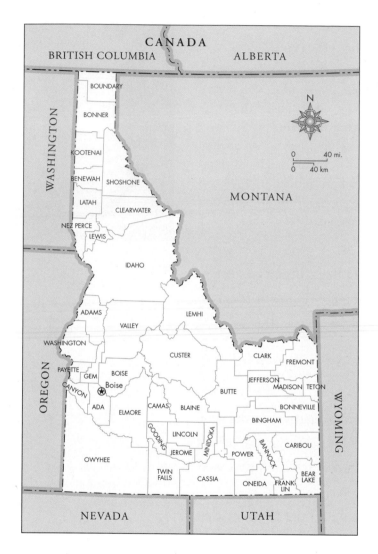

Idaho's counties

justice and four associate justices, all of whom are elected to six-year terms. The chief justice is chosen for a four-year term by members of the court.

The court of appeals is the next highest court in the state. Three judges sit on this court for six-year terms. District judges are elected by voters from seven judicial districts to serve four-year terms. In addition, each county is entitled to at least one magistrate.

Local Government

Idaho is divided into forty-four counties. Three elected commissioners conduct each county's business. Two of these commissioners serve two-year terms, while the third serves a four-year term. The three commissioners decide which of them will head the commission. The sheriff, tax assessor, prosecuting attorney, coroner, treasurer/tax collector, and district court clerk/auditor/recorder are the other county officials. None of these officers may serve more than two terms. Almost all of Idaho's cities have a mayor-city council form of government.

Idaho's State Flag and Seal

The original Idaho state flag was patterned after the battle flag used by the First Idaho Infantry in the Philippines in 1898 during the Spanish-American War. This state flag featured the Idaho territorial seal on a blue field, with the regiment's name beneath the seal. On March 12, 1907, a silk flag was created with a blue field and the state seal in the center.

Embroidered in gold block letters below the seal on a red band were the words *State of Idaho.* This flag was kept on display in the state capitol until it became ragged from wear. A fourth-grade class from Meridian raised $5,000 to have the flag restored so that it could be put on permanent display at the Idaho Historical Museum in Boise.

Symbolizing the major industries in Idaho—forestry and agriculture—and the incredible beauty of the state, the state seal was created in 1890 by Emma Edwards Green. The Idaho seal is the only state seal in the United States designed by a woman. The seal was adopted on March 14, 1891, by the first state legislature, in Boise. Rising above the shield on the seal, the elk's head represents the protection of elk and deer in the state. Also on the seal are the state flower—the white syringa—the state's largest river—the Snake —and the state's motto *Esto Perpetua*, which means "Let it be perpetual" in Latin. ■

National Political Involvement

In 1892, Idaho participated for the first time in a national presidential election. In that election, the majority of votes in the state were cast for the Populist Party. In half of all other presidential elections, a majority of Idahoans have voted for Republican candidates. Idaho's voters have elected more Republicans than Democrats to the U.S. Congress. In spite of their heavy record of voting for Republicans, Idahoans tend to vote for individuals rather than parties.

Idaho's State Symbols

State bird: Mountain bluebird In 1931, the mountain bluebird (left) was selected as the state bird. This bird has bright blue feathers and is about 7 inches (18 cm) long.

State horse: Appaloosa The 1975 legislature designated the Appaloosa, a horse bred by the Nez Perce Indians, the state horse. These beautiful horses can be recognized by their solid color everywhere except on the rump, which is spotted.

State gem: Star garnet The 1967 legislature chose the star garnet as the state gem. The "star" in the garnet has four rays and seems to float on the surface of the stone. Occasionally, a stone is found with six rays. Star garnets are generally dark purple or plum in color.

State tree: Western white pine Since 1935, the western white pine has been the state tree of Idaho. The wood of this tree has a straight grain and soft, even texture. Idaho's state tree, found most plentifully in the northern part of the state, also provides wonderful shade.

State fish: Cutthroat trout In 1990, the cutthroat trout was chosen as the state fish. Its name comes from the red slashes under the jaw that give it the appearance of having had its throat cut.

State flower: White Syringa The beautiful white syringa (below) has been the state flower since 1931. Also called mock orange, the syringa shrub has short, leafy branches that produce clusters of fragrant white blossoms with four petals.

Idaho's State Song
"Here We Have Idaho"

Words by McKinley Helm and Albert J. Tompkins
Music by Sallie Hume-Douglas

The song, originally called "Garden of Paradise," was part of a contest. McKinley Helm, a University of Idaho student, wrote a verse to "Garden of Paradise" and won first place. He called the song "Our Idaho," and it became the school song. In 1931, the title was changed again to "Here We Have Idaho" after it was chosen as the state song by the Idaho legislature.

And here we have Idaho
Winning her way to fame.
Silver and gold in the sunlight
*   blaze,*
And romance lies in her name.

Singing, we're singing of you,
Ah, proudly, too; all our lives
*   through,*
We'll go singing, singing of you,
Singing of Idaho.

There's truly one state in this
*   great land of ours,*
Where ideals can be realized.
The pioneers made it so for you
*   and me,*

A legacy we'll always prize.

CHAPTER EIGHT

Idahoans at Work

daho's economy is closely tied to the land and its resources. Manufacturing, agriculture, tourism, service industries, timber, and mining are Idaho's most important industries. All depend heavily on natural resources. The twentieth century brought prosperity to the Gem State through the wise use of natural resources to enhance the quality of life.

Idaho is blessed with abundant natural resources. The state has rivers and underground water supplies, lumber from forests, mineral wealth from the mountains, and fertile soil. The creativity and independence of Idaho's entrepreneurs also fuel the state's economic success.

The Bitterroot Wilderness, one of Idaho's prized natural areas

Opposite: A canola field near Grangeville

Manufacturing

Manufacturing, once relatively unimportant compared to the production of raw materials, is now Idaho's leading industry. Electrical equipment, machinery, and food production, particularly potato processing, all contribute to the state's economy. Nearly half of Idaho's potato production involves quick-freezing or dehydrating.

Another of Idaho's manufacturing successes involves lumber and wood products, such as plywood, veneers, pulp and paper, furniture, boxes, and railroad ties. Boise-Cascade, a wood-products manufacturer, is headquartered in the capital city.

Other manufacturing includes construction of mobile homes and prefabricated houses. Sheet metal and a variety of structural metals are produced in the Panhandle. Other manufactured goods range from rubber and plastic items to farming and mining equipment.

Hauling logs to the Boise-Cascade lumber mill

Ore-Ida Tater Tots

Nephi and Golden Grigg, brothers from Nampa, founded their business in 1934. They hauled products from farms in Idaho and Oregon south into California and other markets. They leased a plant in 1949 to quick-freeze corn on the cob. Eventually, with an ample supply of potatoes, they tried quick-freezing potatoes too. In 1952, they founded Ore-Ida Potato Products, Inc.

Raw potatoes were processed at the plant, quick-frozen, then stored until shipped all over the country—the beginning of frozen french fries. In 1953, they developed a new product called Tater Tots. These small, round, bite-sized portions of shredded potatoes could be deep-fried or baked, and people loved them.

Ore-Ida merged with the H. J. Heinz Company in 1965. Their products include frozen cookies, pizzas, and vegetables, but 75 percent of their business is frozen potatoes. ■

Farming and the Potato

In Idaho, crops provide most of the agricultural income. Croplands make up just over half the farmland. The remainder is pastureland or rangeland.

Potatoes are Idaho's leading crop. In fact, the state grows almost one-third of the U.S. potato crop. Farmers raise potatoes in the south-central and southeastern sections of the Snake River plain.

Blackfoot, northwest of Pocatello, calls itself the Potato Capital of the World. Idaho is famous for a special potato called the Russet Burbank. It was developed by Luther Burbank, a pioneer in plant experimentation, who produced the original seedlings in the early 1870s.

Idaho farmers also produce milk, beef cattle, sheep, barley, and sugar beets. Truck crops—fruits and vegetables—are grown

Sugar beet farming

in the Lewiston area, as well as in the southwestern part of the state.

Herding sheep in Sun Valley

Small family farms and cattle and sheep ranches are scattered throughout the state. However, large corporate farms account for the majority of Idaho's agricultural sales, both crops and livestock.

What Idaho Grows, Manufactures, and Mines

Agriculture	Manufacturing	Mining
Barley	Electrical equipment	Gold
Beef cattle	Food products	Phosphate rock
Milk	Machinery	Silver
Potatoes	Wood products	
Sugar beets		

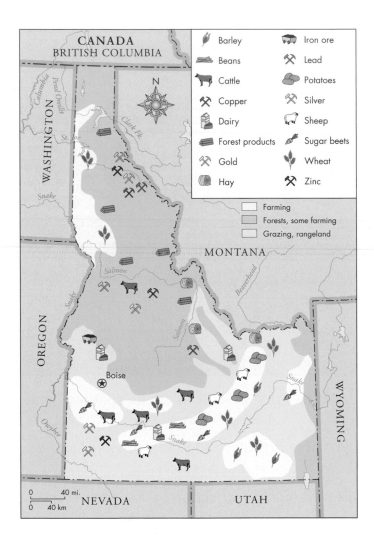

Idaho's natural resources

Tourism

An increasingly important industry to Idaho's economy is tourism. The state's mountains, lakes, waterfalls, wildlife, and plains attract hunters, fishers, and sightseers eager to experience some of the most beautiful scenery on Earth. Skiers, campers, and white-water rafters seek snowcapped peaks, forests, and rivers.

J. R. Simplot and Idaho Potatoes

Born in Iowa in 1909, John Richard Simplot moved with his family to Idaho when he was two years old. They settled on a farm near Declo, and his experiences as a young man led Simplot to try his hand at raising potatoes. He sorted potatoes for a local firm to earn extra money. Then he bought pigs and used rejected potatoes to feed them. Before long, he became a major rancher and feedlot operator on the Snake River plain.

By the end of World War II, Simplot was the largest shipper of dehydrated potatoes in the state. He owned and operated a million-dollar fertilizer plant at Pocatello. In 1957, Simplot convinced Ray Kroc to try frozen french fries in his chain of McDonald's restaurants. Since then, 80 percent of the french fries sold at McDonald's restaurants around the world have come from J. R. Simplot in Boise. Simplot's plants process millions of pounds of potatoes every day— more than any other company in the world.

Simplot has been declared the richest man in Idaho by *Fortune* magazine. Cattle, computer chips, fertilizer, mining, and wool are other enterprises included in his business endeavors. At the age of ninety, Simplot serves as director emeritus for all his companies. His nickname in Boise is Mr. Spud. He and his wife, Esther, are avid supporters of the arts, as well as of Idaho's economy. They contribute to the American Festival Ballet, the Boise Art Museum, and the Boise Opera.

J. R. Simplot once said, "You bet on your judgment—then take what comes, do the best you can with what you've got, and let things grow." He believes in the free-enterprise system, loves the land, and strives for excellence in everything he does. His employees display a loyalty to their boss that is unusual in large companies. ■

Tourism brought in $1.9 billion for the state in 1996. In addition to the actual dollars tourists spend in Idaho, they also provide income for various service industries, including recreation, retail trade, and real estate.

Potato Salad

Potatoes are Idaho's biggest and most famous product.

Ingredients:

3 pounds new Idaho potatoes, peeled

1 cup mayonnaise

3 tablespoons mustard

1 cup very thinly sliced red onion

¼ cup minced chives

salt and pepper to taste

Directions:
Boil the potatoes until tender, about 20 or 30 minutes. Drain the cooked potatoes and place them in cold water until they are no longer too hot to touch.
Then, cut the potatoes in half or in quarters into a large bowl. Mix in mayonnaise, mustard, onions, and chives. Season with salt and pepper. Place in the refrigerator to chill for at least an hour before serving.

Service Industries

The majority of the total value of goods and services produced within Idaho comes from its service industries. A service industry is a business that provides goods or services to the residents of the state. The most important service industries in Idaho are retail and wholesale stores. Products sold wholesale—in large quantities to retailers for resale—include wood products, groceries, and petroleum. Retail businesses include food stores, restaurants, automobile dealerships, and department stores.

The service industries are primarily located in cities and towns. Albertson's, one of the largest U.S. supermarket chains, has its headquarters in Boise.

Banking, insurance, and real estate are important parts of Idaho's service industries. Boise is the center of these businesses. Other service industries in Idaho include community, business, and personal services such as ski resorts, law firms, and some hospitals.

The government also runs important service industries for Idaho. These industries include public education, police and fire protection, road maintenance, public hospitals, and services on Native American reservations. The U.S. government also owns and manages vast tracts of timber and mining land in the mountains.

Joe Albertson (1906–1993)

Born in Oklahoma, Joe Albertson and his family moved to Idaho and settled in Caldwell when Joe was three years old. He attended the College of Idaho and worked as a janitor while getting an education. The job didn't provide enough money for Joe to continue his schooling, however, so he left college and worked as a clerk in a grocery store.

Joe opened his own grocery store in 1939 in Boise. His specialty was "Big Joe" ice cream cones. In time, Albertson's grew into a supermarket chain. Remembering the days he spent as a student at the College of Idaho, Joe gave money and time to help the college. In 1991, the school was renamed Albertson College in his honor. ■

Mining and Minerals

Since the discovery of gold and silver in the 1800s, mining has been an important part of the state's economy. Although its role has diminished since the nineteenth century, mining silver, phosphate rock (for fertilizer), gold, lead, and zinc is still profitable in Idaho. Mining employs several thousand workers statewide. Most precious metals come from the Coeur d'Alene area. Idaho produces about 12 percent of the silver mined in the United States.

Crushed stone, sand, gravel, pumice, and a porous material called perlite are also mined in Idaho. These products, used in the construction industry, add millions of dollars to Idaho's economy each year.

A miner at Sierra Silver Mine

Other Industries

The state's manufacturing, timber, agriculture, and mining industries require support from other industries. The state produces electric power, maintains a good transportation system, and supports various segments of the communications industry.

Most of Idaho's electric power comes from its hydroelectric plants. Even though they generate some 12 billion kilowatt-hours of electricity each year, these projects tap only a small percentage of the state's hydroelectric potential. Public and private utilities include facilities at Dworshak Dam and the Hells Canyon Project, which includes the Brownlee, Oxbow, and Hells Canyon Dams.

Hells Canyon Dam is part of the Hells Canyon Project.

Idaho's transportation system is one of the nation's best. Two major highway systems—Interstate 84 in the southern part of Idaho and Interstate 90 in the north—cross the state east to west. Four transcontinental railroads serve the state, and Lewiston and the larger southern cities have airports with major airline service.

Idahoans keep up with local, national, and world news through about sixty-five newspapers, including one dozen dailies. Boise's *Idaho Statesman*, the *Post-Register* of Idaho Falls, and Pocatello's *Idaho State Journal* are the state's largest newspapers. Idahoans

An Amtrak train arriving in Boise

also get information and entertainment from a variety of radio and television stations.

People around the world watch television thanks to the invention of one famous Idahoan—Philo T. Farnsworth (1906–1971). He produced the first all-electronic television image when he was twenty years old. His invention, Television System, was filed with the U.S. Patent Office on January 7, 1927, and led to the development of modern telecommunications. In addition to the television system, Farnsworth held the patents for the cathode-ray tube and more than 300 other inventions. He was inducted into the National Inventors Hall of Fame in 1984.

CHAPTER NINE

Divided We Stand

A farmer's market near the Grove in Boise

Throughout the history of the state, Idahoans have been extremely independent, yet fiercely loyal to their communities and their state. Whenever necessary, they work toward a common goal—as long as that goal promises to be beneficial to their particular region of the state. Each year brings numerous opportunities for Idahoans to join hands in shared pursuits and celebrate the traditions that bind them, rather than debating issues that divide them.

Population

According to the 1990 census, Idaho's population is 1,011,986. Among the fifty states, Idaho ranks forty-second in population. In 1997 government estimates, the population had grown 20 percent,

Opposite: Near Hyde Park in Boise

Population of Idaho's Major Cities (1990)	
Boise	125,738
Pocatello	46,080
Idaho Falls	43,929
Nampa	28,365
Lewiston	28,082
Twin Falls	27,591

Idaho Falls is one of Idaho's largest cities.

to 1,210,232, raising its rank among the states to fortieth. Idaho's population density is only 12 persons per square mile (5 per sq km).

Towns with more than 5,000 inhabitants are home to 60 percent of Idaho's citizens. Most of these twenty-two towns stand along the Snake River.

Boise, the state's capital and largest city, is home to more than 125,000 of the state's citizens and is Idaho's only designated metropolitan area. It is the only Idaho city with more than 50,000 people. Idaho Falls and Pocatello have populations higher than 40,000, while Lewiston, Nampa, and Twin Falls have more than 25,000 residents.

Ethnic Origins

Only Native Americans lived in Idaho before 1800. After the Lewis and Clark expedition, many gold prospectors, fur traders, and missionaries came to the state, along with Mormons from Utah in the 1850s and 1860s.

Lush forests and fertile farmlands drew Scandinavian immigrants to northern Idaho. In the 1930s, farmers migrated from Texas, Oklahoma, Kansas, and other states affected by severe drought.

The majority of Idahoans are white descendants of English, Irish, and Scottish settlers who came from the Midwest and the East Coast. Other Idahoans have Danish, French, German, and Swedish ancestors and strive to retain that influence in their lives. Native Americans are still an important part of the population, with a little more than 1 percent of the total population, according to 1990 figures.

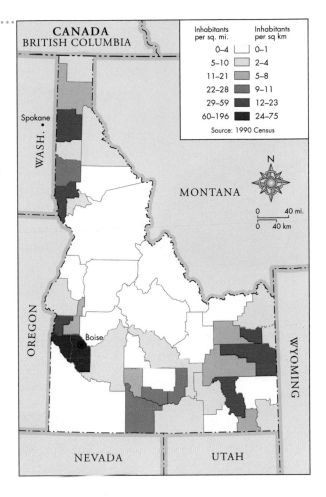

Idaho's population density

Today, Idahoans include a small but growing population of Asians—about 1 percent of the population. Some of their ancestors were included in the approximately 10,000 Japanese Americans interred in relocation centers during World War II. Some are descended from Chinese gold and silver miners. The most recent Asian immigrants came from Southeast Asia, specifically Cambodia, Laos, and Vietnam. Many of Idaho's Asian Americans work in the state's food industries.

Joseph Garry, Coeur D'Alene Tribal Leader (1910–1976)

Born on the Coeur D'Alene Reservation in Idaho, Joseph Garry (left) served as chair of his tribe for twenty years. He also served as president of the largest Native American group in the nation—the National Congress of American Indians. Garry was elected state representative in 1956, becoming the first Native American to serve in the Idaho legislature. He twice earned the title of Outstanding Indian of North America. ■

Idaho's African-American population has never exceeded 1 percent. Most blacks live in the Boise and Pocatello areas. The largest minority in the state is Hispanic, about 5 percent of the population. Many are Basques—descendants of Spaniards from

Young Idahoans

Dancers at a Basque festival

northern Spain. These Basques herded sheep in the Pyrenees Mountains, between France and Spain. The southwest corner of Idaho is home to the highest concentration of Basques in the United States and the largest Basque colony in the world outside the Pyrenees.

Pete Cenarrusa, a Basque (1917–)

In 1917, Pete Cenarrusa was born in Carey to Basque immigrants. Cenarrusa graduated from the University of Idaho and taught in the public schools until he became a marine pilot in World War II. After retiring from the marines, Major Cenarrusa turned to farming and ranching and then was elected to the Idaho house of representatives. He served nine consecutive terms, three of them as speaker of the house.

Cenarrusa was appointed Idaho's secretary of state in 1967, when the former secretary, Edson Deal, died. He has retained that office, becoming the longest-serving official in Idaho's history. In his eighties, he continues to dedicate his time and talents to the people of Idaho. ■

**C. K. Ah-Fong
(1844–1927)**

In the 1860s, C. K. Ah-Fong left his native China and settled near Boise to practice as a physician. He earned his license from the territory and specialized in herbal remedies. Physicians were scarce, and Fong's patients, both Asian and Caucasian, appreciated his skills. ■

Education

The governing body for Idaho schools is the state board of education. The governor appoints seven members to the state school board for five-year terms. The head of Idaho's school system is the state superintendent of public instruction, who is elected to a four-year term. In 1946, Idaho's 1,100 districts were consolidated into more than 100 districts.

The earliest schools in the state were missionary schools established to educate and convert local American Indians. Henry Spalding established the first school for Native American children in Idaho at the Lapwai Mission in 1837. In 1860, Mormons founded in Franklin the first school for white children in the state. Idaho's first high school was established in Boise in 1882.

In 1890, Congress designated two large pieces of land in each township for schools. Very little of this land was actually used for schools, but income from the land—mainly property taxes—still goes toward education. Idaho schools are supported through taxation. In 1965, Idaho's legislature passed a state sales tax earmarked for education to supplement property-tax revenue.

Idaho has six public and six private institutions of higher learning. Chartered in 1889, the University of Idaho, at Moscow, is the foremost state university, with approximately 10,000 students. Three schools offer four-year degree programs—Idaho State University at Pocatello, Boise State University, and Lewis-Clark State College at Lewiston. Idaho's private colleges include Albertson College, formerly the College of Idaho, at Caldwell (a Presbyterian institution), Northwest Nazarene College at Nampa, and Ricks College at Rexburg (a Mormon junior college).

Boise State University is located along the Boise River.

Libraries

Idaho has a wealth of libraries, including more than 100 public libraries. Boise Public Library is Idaho's largest library. The State Law Library, founded in 1869 and located in Boise, houses Idaho's largest legal collection. The University of Idaho Library houses important titles in northwest Americana, as well as unique Basque materials. Idaho State Historical Museum in Boise is the official depository for state records as well as for Idaho's historical manuscripts and newspapers.

Museums

Idaho has a variety of museums. In Boise, the Idaho State Historical Society operates a museum devoted to state history. The Boise Art Museum, founded in 1937, features a prestigious collection of American realist paintings as well as the work of local artists. The

Herrett Museum in Twin Falls, on the campus of the College of Southern Idaho, displays an impressive collection of pre-Columbian artifacts, Hopi kachina dolls, gems and minerals, and a variety of art.

The Idaho Museum of Natural History, on the Idaho State University campus in Pocatello, has exhibits on Idaho's geologic history and displays specimens of Idaho flora and fauna. Craters of the Moon National Monument Museum in Arco has exhibits on geology and natural history. The Idaho Historical Society publishes a quarterly journal, *Idaho Yesterdays*.

The Boise Art Museum boasts a fine collection of American paintings.

Churches

In 1834, the Methodist Episcopal Church in Fort Hall held the first church service in Idaho. Mormons, Catholics, and Presbyterians followed Methodist Episcopals into the state. Today, prominent religious denominations in Idaho include Mormons, Roman Catholics, Baptists, and Methodists.

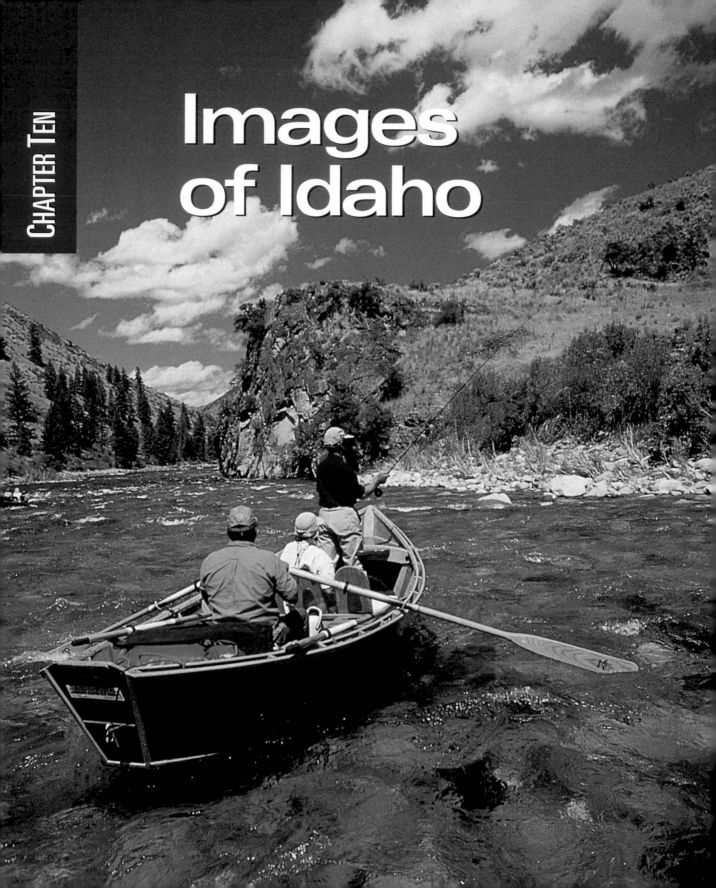

CHAPTER TEN

Images
of Idaho

M ost Idahoans would say their state is a work of art—from the rugged sculpture of its mountain ranges to the sweeping flow of its rivers and the thunder of its waterfalls. Such sights and sounds have inspired the state's artists and writers for more than a century.

Idaho is known for its Native American crafts.

Arts and Crafts

Idaho's artists are talented in many areas besides drawing, painting, and sculpture. Museums, private homes, county fairs, and folk-art exhibitions display hand-tooled leather saddles and wrought-iron gates and fences as well as quilts and embroidery.

Native American crafts are popular, with baskets and beadwork, decorated cradleboards, horsehair bridles, duck decoys, tablecloths,

Opposite: Fishing the Salmon River

rag rugs, and parfleches (bags made of dried rawhide soaked in lye and stripped of hair). Idaho is home to tinsmiths, furniture makers, needleworkers, quilt makers, potters, carvers, and engravers.

Boise began hosting art exhibits in the 1870s at territorial and state fairs. The Lewis and Clark Exposition in Portland in 1905, the Alaska-Yukon-Pacific Exposition in Seattle in 1909, the Panama-Pacific International Exposition in San Francisco in 1915, the Century of Progress at Chicago, in 1933–34, and the New York World's Fair in 1939, all had important contributions from Idaho artists.

The state's most noted artist was Gutzon Borglum, who sculpted the presidential portraits on Mount Rushmore in South Dakota. Borglum worked on the project for fourteen years but died before the figures were completely finished. The monument was completed by his son, Lincoln Borglum.

Gutzon Borglum (1867–1941)

Born in a log cabin in Ovid, Idaho, in 1867, Gutzon Borglum was the son of Danish immigrants. Gutzon later lived in Utah, Nebraska, and Missouri, but some of his relatives remained in Idaho. As an adult, Gutzon studied art in San Francisco and Paris, and had his own studio in London. He gained international fame as a sculptor. In 1901, he settled in New York City.

In 1927, Borglum was commissioned to carve the busts of Presidents Washington, Lincoln, Jefferson, and Theodore Roosevelt on the granite face of Mount Rushmore in South Dakota. The accomplishment remains one of the most remarkable achievements in American sculpture. President Calvin Coolidge dedicated the monument on August 10, 1927. The sculpture was unveiled in sections between 1930 and 1939. Gutzon Borglum died in 1941. ■

Writers

Lewis and Clark's journals provided the first writings about Idaho. Since then, talented authors have written about the state's history, people, and landscape. Novels, folktales, legends, magazines, newspapers, and state histories have contributed significantly to U.S. history and literature.

Annie Pike Greenwood, author of *We Sagebrush Folks*

Women writers such as Annie Pike Greenwood, Nelle Davis, Inez Puckett McEwen, and Grace Jordan contributed personal accounts of the life and hardships of living in Idaho. Greenwood's *We Sagebrush Folks* tells about the settlement and development near the Minidoka Dam and recounts the daily life of farm families in southern Idaho.

Nelle Davis's book *Stump Ranch Pioneer* tells about refugees in the Idaho Panhandle during the Dust Bowl days of the 1930s. McEwen's book *So This Is Ranching* is a humorous overview of ranch life in southern Idaho in the 1940s. Jordan's book *Home Below Hells Canyon* records the Jordan family's experiences as sheep ranchers in the 1930s and 1940s.

Idaho authors of fiction include Mary Hallock Foote, Frank Robertson, Ridley Pearson, and Ezra Pound—a world-renowned poet, translator, and literary critic. More has been written about Pound than about any other Idaho writer. He is always introduced as Idaho-born.

Idaho has also produced authors of fiction for children and young adults, including Carol Ryrie Brink, who won the Newbery

Ezra Pound (1885–1972)

Born in Hailey in 1885, Ezra Pound lived there two years, before his family moved to Pennsylvania. After graduating from the University of Pennsylvania, Pound taught at Wabash College until he went to Europe in 1908. In Italy, he published *A Lume Spento*, his first volume of poetry. In London, he published three more volumes of verse and co-founded the imagist school of poets, advocating the use of free rhythms and concrete images.

Pound promoted the work of two writers—James Joyce and T. S. Eliot. In 1920, Pound moved to Paris where he joined a group of Americans, including Gertrude Stein and Ernest Hemingway, whom he influenced greatly.

In 1924, Pound moved to Italy. He partially supported the programs of Italian premiere Benito Mussolini and was charged with treason by the United States in 1945. He was ruled insane and spent twelve years in a mental hospital. He was released in 1958 and died in 1972. ■

Medal for *Caddie Woodlawn* in 1936. Janet Campbell Hale and Christine Quintasket, whose pen name was Mourning Dove, or Hum-ishu-ma, also came from Idaho. Quintasket was the one of the first Native American woman novelists.

Perhaps the most famous writer to live in Idaho was Ernest Hemingway. Born in Illinois in 1889, he first came to Ketchum, Idaho, in 1939. Twenty years later, he left his home in Cuba when Fidel Castro came to power and moved to Idaho, where he lived until his death in 1961.

Winner of the Pulitzer Prize for literature in 1953 for *The Old Man and the Sea* and the Nobel Prize for literature in 1954, "Papa" Hemingway considered Idaho unspoiled. He once said of a high switchback—a sharply winding road—on Old Summit Road above

Ernest Hemingway (1899–1961)

Born in Oak Park, Illinois, in 1899, Ernest Hemingway never attended college. Instead, he worked as a newspaperman and traveled extensively, making frequent trips to Spain and the Austrian Alps. For the most part, though, he lived in Paris.

Hemingway's first published work was *Three Stories and Ten Poems* (1923). His first novel, *Torrents of Spring* (1926), was a satire. He returned to the United States in 1927, but covering the Spanish Civil War in 1936 inspired him to write *For Whom the Bell Tolls* (1940), which he finished while living in Idaho. After the war, his short novel *The Old Man and the Sea* (1952) earned him the Pulitzer Prize for literature in 1953. A year later, he won the Nobel Prize.

In his last years, Hemingway suffered physical ailments, mental depression, and paranoia. He committed suicide at his home in Ketchum, Idaho, on July 2, 1961. Ernest Hemingway is considered one of the world's major literary figures of the twentieth century.

The Ernest Hemingway Memorial, located northeast of Ketchum on Trail Creek Road, features photographs and memorabilia of Hemingway's years in Idaho. ■

the River of No Return, "You'd have to come from a test tube and think like a machine not to engrave all of this in your head so that you never lose it."

Hemingway loved Idaho. He once wrote a tribute that was carved to a friend on his stone memorial, overlooking Trail Creek near Sun Valley: "Best of all he loved the fall/The leaves yellow on the cottonwoods/Leaves floating on the trout streams/And above the hills/The high blue windless skies/. . . now he will be a part of them/Forever." Hemingway's wife, Mary, called Idaho "Papa's Country."

Idaho has produced numerous nonfiction writers, including

several renowned historians. Their diaries, letters, reminiscences, and personal histories recount the early days of the Gem State. Two have earned Pulitzer Prizes for historical writing—Lawrence Henry Fipson in 1962 and Laurel Thatcher Ulrich in 1991.

Some of the best histories of Idaho have been written recently. F. Ross Peterson, Carlos Schwantes, Dwight William Jensen, and Leonard J. Arrington have all chronicled the state's history in volumes that convey the intense pride, individualism, and tradition of Idahoans.

Entertainers

Idaho has been home to two movie stars—Lana Turner and Mariel Hemingway. Lana Turner was born Julia Turner in Wallace, in 1920. At the age of fifteen, she went to Hollywood, was discovered while drinking a soda at a local drugstore, and signed a movie contract. She became one of the world's most glamorous stars. Lana Turner is best known for her roles in the films *Ziegfeld Girl*, *The Postman Always Rings Twice*, and *Peyton Place*.

Mariel Hemingway, the granddaughter of author Ernest Hemingway, was born in Mill Valley, Idaho, in 1961.

Movie star Lana Turner was born in Wallace.

She starred in the popular movies *Manhattan*, *Personal Best*, and *Falling from Grace*.

Mariel Hemingway was born in Mill Valley.

A State of Sports Lovers

Outdoor sports abound in Idaho, with hunting, fishing, skiing, backpacking, and camping popular among residents and tourists alike. Experienced guides lead exciting raft trips through Hells Canyon and along the Salmon River. Hunters pursue deer, bear, elk, pheasant, partridge, and duck in mountain forests and on the plains. Fishing enthusiasts catch salmon, trout, and whitefish in the state's rushing streams and quiet lakes.

Idaho is also a skier's paradise. Sun Valley, home to the world's first ski lift and Idaho's best-known ski resort, lies 6,000 feet (1,830 m) above sea level. Other Idaho resorts include Bogus Basin, near Boise; Brundage, near McCall; Schweitzer, near Sandpoint; Silver Mountain, near Coeur d'Alene; Pebble Creek, near Pocatello; and Grand Targhee, near Driggs.

In the field of athletics, Idaho has produced its share of heroes. Every high school and college athletic team has its loyal and enthusiastic fans, and keen competition exists in football, basketball, baseball, track and field, and rodeo. Several professional athletes have also called Idaho their home.

Skiing in Sun Valley

Picabo Street

Picabo Street was born in 1971 in a hippie commune and was named for the tiny village of Picabo (pronounced peek-a-boo), Idaho. She won the silver medal in women's downhill racing at the 1994 winter Olympics in Lillehammer, Norway. But in 1996, Street badly injured her left knee during training in Vail, Colorado. Many wondered if her career might be over. At the 1998 winter Olympics in Nagano, Japan, however, she battled back to win a gold medal in the Super G. Street, who lives in Hailey and skis at Sun Valley, hopes to overcome her injuries to compete in the 2002 winter Olympics in Salt Lake City. ■

Football Players

Jerry Kramer, born in Montana in 1936, grew up in Idaho and attended high school in Sand-point and then played for the University of Idaho Vandals. He joined the National Football League (NFL) in 1958 and played offensive lineman and kicker for Coach Vince Lombardi's Green Bay Packers.

Jerry Kramer lived in Idaho and played for the University of Idaho before joining the NFL.

Kramer was named All-Pro five times, helping the Packers win five national championships. Since retiring from professional football, Kramer has written several books about his experiences, including *Farewell to Football*, in 1969. He lives in Parma, Idaho.

Larry Wilson, born on March 24, 1938, in Rigby, was drafted by the St. Louis Cardinals in 1960 and played defensive back until 1972. He was twice chosen the team's Most Valuable Player. In 1966, he was also named NFL Defensive Player of the Year. Wilson was selected All-NFL five times and played in eight Pro Bowl games.

Wilson was known as the "toughest man in football," once playing a game with two broken hands. He was elected to the Pro Football Hall of Fame in 1978. On January 31, 1999, he was selected for the All-Millennium Team.

Two members of the Super Bowl XXXIII champion Denver Broncos—Mark Schlereth and Marvin Washington—played at the

University of Idaho. Schlereth, left guard, came to Denver in 1995, after leaving the Washington Redskins. As a Redskin, he was named to the Pro Bowl in 1991. In 1997, he was named to the *Sports Illustrated* All-NFL team. During his ten-year career in the NFL, Marvin Washington played defensive end for the San Francisco Forty-Niners and the New York Jets before joining the Broncos.

Baseball great Walter Johnson grew up in Weiser.

Baseball Players

Three of the best players in professional baseball came from Idaho—Walter Johnson, Vernon Law, and Harmon Killebrew. Johnson grew up in Weiser, Law was born in Meridian, and Killebrew came from Payette.

Often called the greatest baseball player of all time, Walter Johnson played in Idaho in 1906. On June 20, Johnson struck out thirteen batters when his Weiser team defeated Emmett. Before his streak ended, Johnson pitched eighty-five innings without allowing a single run, striking out 166 men. The "Weiser Wonder" signed with the American League's Washington Senators in 1907.

Johnson pitched for the Senators for twenty-one years. He set the major-league record for strikeouts (3,509) and still holds the record for shutouts (110). Johnson's fastball was considered the fastest of all time and earned him the nickname Big Train.

Johnson was one of the first five players inducted into the National Baseball Hall of Fame in 1936.

Vernon Law, born in 1930, pitched sixteen seasons for the Pittsburgh Pirates in the National League and won 162 games. In 1960, he received the Cy Young Award as major-league baseball's best pitcher.

Harmon Killebrew was born on June 29, 1936. He led the American League's Minnesota Twins to three championships and won six league home-run crowns. Killebrew was inducted into the National Baseball Hall of Fame in 1984.

A Rodeo Star

Jackson Sundown was a Nez Perce horseman from central Idaho. In 1916, at the age of fifty, he competed against men half his age in the World Saddle Bronc Riding Championship, won the competition, and became the only Native American to win that title. He died in 1923.

Jackson Sundown won the 1916 World Saddle Bronc Riding Championship.

Timeline

United States History

The first permanent English settlement is established in North America at Jamestown. **1607**

Pilgrims found Plymouth Colony, the second permanent English settlement. **1620**

America declares its independence from Britain. **1776**

The Treaty of Paris officially ends the Revolutionary War in America. **1783**

The U.S. Constitution is written. **1787**

The Louisiana Purchase almost doubles the size of the United States. **1803**

The United States and Britain fight the War of 1812. **1812–15**

The North and South fight each other in the American Civil War. **1861–65**

Idaho State History

1805 The Lewis and Clark expedition crosses through Idaho on its way to the Pacific coast.

1809 David Thompson builds first fur-trading post in Idaho.

1834 Fort Hall and Fort Boise are established.

1860 Gold is discovered on Orofino Creek.

United States History

The United States is **1917-18** involved in World War I.

The stock market crashes, **1929** plunging the United States into the Great Depression.

The United States **1941-45** fights in World War II.
The United States becomes a **1945** charter member of the U.N.

The United States **1951-53** fights in the Korean War.

The U.S. Congress enacts a series of **1964** groundbreaking civil rights laws.

The United States **1964-73** engages in the Vietnam War.

The United States and other **1991** nations fight the brief Persian Gulf War against Iraq.

Idaho State History

1863 Idaho becomes a U.S. territory.

1877 U.S. troops defeat the Nez Perce in the Nez Perce War.

1890 Idaho becomes the forty-third state on July 3.

1905 Former governor Frank Steunenberg is murdered.

1955 Arco, Idaho, becomes the first town in the world to be powered completely by nuclear energy for one hour on July 17.

1972 Ninety-one miners die in a fire at the Sunshine Mine in Kellogg.

1988 The Idaho state lottery is approved.

1992 Three people are killed in a standoff between federal agents and survivalist Randy Weaver at Ruby Ridge.

Fast Facts

State capitol

Mountain bluebird

Statehood date	July 3, 1890, the 43rd state
Origin of state name	Believed to mean "gem of the mountains" or "it is sun-up!"
State capital	Boise
State nickname	The Gem State
State motto	*Esto Perpetua* (Let it be perpetual)
State bird	Mountain bluebird
State horse	Appaloosa
State fish	Cutthroat trout
State flower	White syringa
State gem	Star garnet

Snake River

State song	"Here We Have Idaho"
State tree	Western white pine
State fair	Boise (late August) and Blackfoot (early September)
Total area; rank	83,574 sq. mi. (216,457 sq km), 14th
Land; rank	82,751 sq. mi. (214,325 sq km), 11th
Water; rank	823 sq. mi. (2,132 sq km), 31st
Inland water; rank	823 sq. mi. (2,132 sq km), 25th
Geographic center	Custer, southwest of Challis
Latitude and longitude	Idaho is located approximately between 42° and 49° N and 113° 03′ and 117° 16′ W
Highest point	Borah Peak 12,662 feet (3,862 m)
Lowest point	710 feet (217 m) at Snake River
Largest city	Boise
Number of counties	44
Population; rank	1,011,986 (1990 census); 42nd
Density	12 persons per sq. mi. (5 per sq km)
Population distribution	57% urban, 43% rural

Ethnic distribution (does not equal 100%)

White	94.41%
Hispanic	5.26%
Other	2.96%
Native American	1.37%
Asian and Pacific Islanders	0.93%
African-American	0.33%

Idahoans

Record high temperature	118°F (48°C) at Orofino on July 28, 1934
Record low temperature	−60°F (−51°C) at Island Park Dam on January 18, 1943
Average July temperature	67°F (19°C)
Average January temperature	23°F (−5°C)
Average annual precipitation	19 inches (48 cm)

Natural Areas

National Park

Yellowstone National Park is America's first national park. It lies primarily in Wyoming and Montana and contains the world's largest geyser fields.

National Monument

Craters of the Moon National Monument has dramatic volcanic cones, caves, and lava fields more than 2,100 years old.

Hagerman Fossil Beds National Monument protects fossils that are embedded in the banks of the Snake River.

National Reserve

City of Rocks National Reserve protects remnants of the California Trail and features dramatic granite spires and sculpted rock formations.

National Historical Park

Nez Perce National Historical Park commemorates the history and culture of the Nez Perce people. Parts of the park are also in Washington, Montana, and Oregon.

Craters of the Moon National Monument

Hells Canyon

National Forests

Idaho is home to ten national forests that cover 20.4 million acres (8.3 million ha)—almost two-fifths of the state's total land area. They include:

Boise National Forest is the largest in the state—and the seventh largest in the nation—and covers more than 2.6 million acres (1 million ha). It is home to wild rivers and a predominantly ponderosa pine and Douglas fir ecosystem.

Caribou National Forest was established by President Theodore Roosevelt in 1903. It covers more than 1 million acres (405,000 ha).

Challis National Forest contains Borah Peak, the highest mountain in Idaho.

Clearwater National Forest contains approximately 1.8 million acres (729,000 ha) of varied mountain scenery and canyons.

Grand Targhee National Forest was formed in 1908 with the consolidation of Henry's Lake Forest Reserve and part of the Yellowstone Reserve. Named for a prominent Bannock Indian leader and signer of the Fort Bridger Treaty of 1868, the forest covers about 1.8 million acres (729,000 ha).

Idaho Panhandle National Forest has some of Idaho's most scenic mountain ranges, including the Selkirk, Cabinet, Coeur d'Alene, and Bitterroot Ranges, as well as three of the state's largest lakes—Pend Oreille, Coeur d'Alene, and Priest Lakes.

Nez Perce National Forest includes Hells Canyon. This gorge on the Snake River is the deepest in North America, dropping more than 8,032 feet (2,450 m).

Payette National Forest, located in west-central Idaho, north of Boise, covers approximately 2.3 million acres (931,500 ha). Protected within its boundaries are lush conifer forests, hot and dry desert grasslands, and snow-covered mountain peaks.

Sawtooth National Forest, established in 1905, covers 2.1 million acres (850,500 ha).

Grand Targhee National Forest

State Parks

Idaho maintains twenty-two areas as parks and recreational sites. They include:

The largest, *Heyburn State Park*, covers 5,505 acres (2,230 ha) in northern Idaho.

Bruneau Dunes State Park has some of the tallest sand dunes in North America.

Part of the Oregon Trail is preserved in *Massacre Rocks State Park*, where pioneers traveling the Oregon Trail carved their names on Register Rock.

Sports Teams

NCAA Teams (Division 1)
Boise State University Broncos

Idaho State University Bengals

University of Idaho Vandals

Cultural Institutions

Libraries
Boise Public Library is Idaho's largest public library.

Idaho State Historical Museum (Boise) is the official depository for state records as well as for Idaho's historical manuscripts and newspapers.

The State Law Library, founded in 1869, houses Idaho's largest legal collection.

Museums
Boise Art Museum, Idaho's leading art museum, contains an important collection of art by Idaho artists. It opened in 1937.

Boise Art Museum

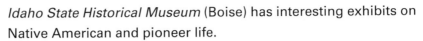

Boise State University campus

Idaho State Historical Museum (Boise) has interesting exhibits on Native American and pioneer life.

Idaho Museum of Natural History (Pocatello) at Idaho State University has anthropology and archaeology exhibits.

Universities and Colleges

In the late 1990s, Idaho had six public and six private institutions of higher learning.

Annual Events

January–March

Sun Valley Winter Carnival (January)

Winter Sports Carnival in McCall (January)

Lionel Hampton Jazz Festival in Moscow (February)

Harriman Cup in Sun Valley (March)

National Circuit Finals Rodeo in Pocatello (March)

April–June

Dogwood Festival in Lewiston (April–May)

Cinco de Mayo in Caldwell (May)

Mat Alyma Powwow and Root Feast in Kamiah (May)

Live History Days in Jerome (June)

Magic Valley Dairy Days in Wendell (June)

Timberfest in Sandpoint (June)

July–September

Diamond Cup hydroplane races on Coeur d'Alene Lake (July)

Snake River Stampede rodeo in Nampa (July)

Shoshone sun dances at Fort Hall Reservation (late July and August)

Western Idaho State Fair in Boise (August)

Dancers at a Basque festival

Picabo Street

Eastern Idaho State Fair in Blackfoot (September)

Lewiston Round-Up in Lewiston (September)

Lumberjack Days in Orofino (September)

October–December

Sun Valley Jazz Jamboree (mid-October)

Festival of Trees in Coeur d'Alene (November)

Silver Valley Arts and Crafts Fall Fair in Osburn (November)

Winter Spirit Festival of Lights in Lewiston (November and December)

Famous People

Ernest Hemingway

Joe Albertson (1906–1993)	Grocery chain founder
William Edgar Borah (1865–1940)	Public official and political leader
Gutzon Borglum (1867–1941)	Sculptor
Carol Ryrie Brink (1895–1981)	Author
Frank Church (1924–1984)	U.S. senator
Henry Dworshak (1894–1962)	U.S. senator
Joseph Garry (1910–1976)	Tribal leader
William D. "Big Bill" Haywood (1869–1928)	Labor leader
Ernest Hemingway (1899–1961)	Author
Mariel Hemingway (1961–)	Actor
Walter Johnson (1887–1946)	Baseball player
Chief Joseph (1840?–1904)	Native American leader
Harmon Killebrew (1936–)	Baseball player
Jerry Kramer (1936–)	Football player
Vernon Law (1930–)	Baseball player

Ezra Loomis Pound (1885–1972)   Poet

Sacajawea (1786?–1812)   Indian guide

J. R. Simplot (1909–)   Industrialist

Jedediah Smith (1799–1831)   Explorer

Picabo Street (1971–)   Downhill skier

Jackson Sundown (1866–1923)   Horseman

Lana Turner (1920–1995)   Actor

Larry Wilson (1938–)   Football player

Lana Turner

To Find Out More

History

- Fradin, Dennis Brindell. *Idaho.* Danbury, Conn.: Children's Press, 1995.
- Kummer, Patricia. *Idaho.* Mankato, Minn.: Capstone Press, 1998.
- Pelta, Kathy. *Idaho.* Minneapolis: Lerner, 1995.
- Thompson, Kathleen. *Idaho.* Austin, Tex.: Raintree/Steck Vaughn, 1996.

Fiction

- Beatty, Patricia. *Bonanza Girl.* New York: William Morrow, 1993.
- Creech, Sharon. *Walk Two Moons.* New York: Harper-Collins Juvenile Books, 1994.
- Hamilton, Morse. *The Garden of Eden Motel.* New York: Greenwillow, 1999.

Biographies

- Kavanagh, Jack. *Walter Johnson.* Broomall, Penn.: Chelsea House, 1992.
- St. George, Judith. *Sacagawea.* New York: Philomel Books, 1997.
- Taylor, Marion W. *Chief Joseph: Nez Perce Leader.* Broomall, Penn.: Chelsea House, 1993.

Websites

■ **State of Idaho**
http://www2.state.id.us/
The official website for
Idaho state government

■ **Idaho State Historical
Society**
*http://www2.state.id.us/
ishs/index.html*
An online guide to the historical society's exhibits, as
well as links to related sites

■ **Idaho Travel and Tourism
Guide**
http://www.visitid.org/
A site supported by the
Idaho Division of Tourism
Development that provides
a guide to Idaho's many
natural and man-made
attractions

Addresses

■ **Idaho Legislature**
Statehouse
Boise, ID 83720
For information on Idaho's
state government

■ **Idaho Department of
Commerce**
P.O. Box 83720
Boise, ID 83720
For information on Idaho's
economy, history, and
tourism

Index

Page numbers in *italics* indicate illustrations.

Meet the
Authors

Charles George received a bachelor's degree in Spanish and history from Tarleton State University in Stephenville, Texas. He taught Spanish and social studies for fifteen years on the high school level, then retired to write full-time. He loves doing research.

Linda George received a bachelor's degree in elementary education from the University of Texas at El Paso. She taught at the elementary school level for ten years. In 1979, she began her professional writing career.

"For the writing of *Idaho*, we gathered stacks of information about the state," explain the Georges. "Then we searched the Internet. But nothing we found portrayed the incredible beauty of the state itself or the warm hospitality of Idaho's people. Whether skiing at Sun Valley during the winter or white-water rafting through Hells Canyon during the summer, we have found Idaho's scenery breathtaking. In fact, photography has always been a favorite hobby of ours and Idaho offers endless opportunities."

Charles and Linda George have written more than thirty nonfiction books for children and young adults, including several titles for Children's Press. They live in central Texas near the small town of Rising Star and spend summers in the cool mountains of New Mexico, near Cloudcroft.

Photo Credits